PUBLICATION DESIGN ANNUAL 23

# ACKNOWLEDGEMENTS

TWENTY-THIRD
PUBLICATION DESIGN ANNUAL

DESIGNERS
Anthony Russell
Samuel Kuo
Anthony Russell, Inc.
New York, NY

2

PHOTOGRAPHER, COVER AND
TITLE PAGES
Ed Eckstein
New York, NY

TYPOGRAPHER
SGW Associates, Inc.
New York, NY

COMPETITION CHAIRPERSON
Mary K. Baumann

CATEGORY CHAIRPERSONS
Melissa Tardiff
Karen M. Bloom
John Belknap
Ron Couture

EXHIBITION COMMITTEE
Phyllis Richmond Cox

CALL FOR ENTRIES DESIGN
Mary K. Baumann
Will Hopkins

SPECIAL THANKS TO
Madison Square Press
New York, NY

Westavco Corporation
New York, NY

Gordonian Printing Co. Inc.
Jersey City, NJ

Anagraphics, Inc.
New York, NY

Compton Press, Inc.
Morris Plains, NJ

New York Times Foundation

Andrea Cobb
Mary Farias
Steve Higgins
Teresa Labiak
Jane Sanders
Susan Weiss

Lina Magazines
New York, NY

OFFICERS
President
Diana La Guardia
*Condé Nast Traveler*

Vice President
Mary K. Baumann
*Will Hopkins Group*

Vice President
Derek Ungless
*Vogue*

Secretary
Amy Bogert
*MS*

Treasurer
Lee Ann Jaffee
Lee Ann Jaffee Design

BOARD OF DIRECTORS
Robert Altemus
Altemus Design

David Armario
*West*

Carla Barr
Calvin Klein Cosmetics

John Belkuap
*7 Days*

Tom Bentkowski
*Life*

Karen Bloom
Westvaco Corporation

Bob Ciano
*Travel and Leisure*

Phyllis Richmond Cox
*Bride's*

Virginia Smith
Baruch College

Melissa Tardiff
*Town & Country*

Mary Zisk
*Creative Ideas*

DIRECTOR:
Bride M. Whelan

DISTRIBUTORS TO THE TRADE IN
THE UNITED STATES AND CANADA
Watson-Guptill
1515 Broadway
New York, NY 10036

DISTRIBUTORS THROUGHOUT THE
REST OF THE WORLD
Hearst Publications International
105 Madison Avenue
New York, NY 10016

PUBLISHER
Madison Square Press, Inc.
10 East 23rd Street
New York, NY 10010

ISBN 0-8230-57-631

ISSN 0885-6370

PRINTED IN JAPAN

# CONTENTS

The Society of Publication Designers is aimed specifically at meeting the needs of editorial art directors and designers across the country. By encouraging a forum among the most accomplished professionals in the field, and by inviting the best of them to judge its competition each year, the Society promotes rigorous standards of achievement in publication design. SPD recognizes the art director in an editorial capacity, as a visual journalist, and honors those who distinguish themselves in this way.

A variety of activities are offered by the Society which include the yearly Competition, the Awards Gala, the Annual, and the Exhibition; a monthly Speaker's Evening brings together distinguished professionals to share their unique contributions to publication design: a bi-monthly newsletter, GRIDS, highlights activities and general information of the Society and the various goings-on amidst the publications community; and the Portfolio Shows, showcases for new editorial illustrators and photographers.

The Society of Publication Designers, founded in 1965, is a non-profit organization.

# PRESIDENT'S LETTER

**Diana La Guardia, art director of *Condé Nast Traveler* and president of the Society of Publication Designers, 1987-88.**

5

Art directors share with editors this most pressing goal: to reach readers. We share this too: the knowledge that a magazine must work hard and fast to this end, given that readers have little time, and many publications to choose from. There is no question but that they are engaged by what they see,

Art directors address the problem of reaching readers by bringing their visual sensibilities into play. We do so not by choosing a pretty typeface, but by maintaining order. We know the architecture of a magazine, and know where a reader expects to find certain information. We encourage editors to use display type in ways that will guide the reader intelligently through the editorial material. We manipulate various elements of design so that the reader can anticipate the specific subject matter even before he begins to read. Art directors work with editors to arrive at a mix

that provides visual variety and pacing. Success here rests on how thoroughly an art director manages to define and convey the editorial focus of a publication.

On the brutally cold weekend of February 6 and 7, 1988, the Board of Directors of the Society of Publication Designers invited a group of most accomplished art directors to judge works published in 1987. I thank them here again for giving their time. This annual contains the award-winning pieces which they voted as the best of the year. By producing it, the SPD honors the collaborative effort between art director and editor, but above all celebrates the art director as visual journalist.
—*Diana LaGuardia*

## CONSUMER CLASSIFICATION

STANDING—L TO R
Lloyd Ziff
*Lloyd Ziff, Inc.*
Nora Sheehan
*Life*
Eric Seidman
*Money*

SEATED
Derek Ungless
*Rolling Stone*
Alexander Isely
*Spy*

# J U D G E S

**6**

## CORPORATE, INSTITUTIONAL AND ANNUAL REPORT CLASSIFICATION

STANDING—L TO R
Anthony Russell
Anthony Russell, Inc.
John Waters
John Waters Associates, Inc.
Bennett Robinson
Corporate Graphics, Inc.

SEATED—L TO R
Peter Harrison
Pentagram, Inc.
John T. Cohoe
*Mercedes*
McCaffrey & McCall, Inc.

## NEWSPAPER AND TABLOID CLASSIFICATION

STANDING – L TO R
Tony Majeri
*Chicago Tribune*
Brock Sears
*Fort Worth Star Telegram*
Linda Brewer
*The New York Times*

SEATED
Lynn Staley
*Boston Globe*
Greg Leeds
*Wall St. Journal*

GREG MILLER

## TRADE CLASSIFICATION

STANDING – L TO R
Shelley Williams
Whittle Communications
Skip Johnston
*PC World*
Traci Churchill
*Money*
Amy Bogert
*MS*

SEATED
Deborah Gallagher Lewis
*Photo / Design*

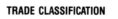

**Frank Zachary is the winner of the 1988 Herb Lubalin Award for
Continuing Excellence in the field of publication design.**

LINDA STILLMAN

The philosopher dispenses wisdom. The teacher dispenses knowledge. The journalist dispenses information. Frank Zachary has stubbornly pursued this principle with uncompromising dedication and excellence.

From the very beginning, he has been an unwavering believer in the photograph as the ultimate form of journalism. He has put his personal stamp on each of his publications with a view of the world that is both true and elegant. He has worn many hats—reporter, photographer, picture editor, art director, editor and conceptualizer. He is the complete editor with a sure instinct for matching the ideal writer with the right photographer.

Zachary started his career in Pittsburgh, working for the newsweekly *Pittsburgh*

*Bulletin-Index,* a pioneering forerunner of the city magazines. After serving as a senior information specialist with the Office of War Information during World War II, working *Victory, USA* and *Photo Review,* his first post-war job took him to *Minicam* magazine, now *Modern Photography.*

In 1948, he proceeded to create and edit *Portfolio,* a quarterly magazine of the graphic arts, working with Alexey Brodovitch as art director. Though only three issues were published, it remains in the international art world as one of the most innovative design magazines ever published in the United States—its format and point of view as contemporary today as 40 years ago.

Following *Portfolio,* Zachary rejoined Curtis in 1951 until 1964 as art director of *Holiday* magazine, which was born in the golden era of picture magazines of the 50s and 60s

and which boasted one million in circulation.

He has recognized the talents of many photographers early in their careers, inspiring them to their full potentials, to create page after page of classically laid-out stories. In all of his endeavors, he has treated his magazines always with a sense of great style, dignity and exceptional taste.

Today, Frank Zachary is editor-in-chief of *Town & Country* magazine, a post he has held for the past 15 years. Under his direction, the magazine has progressed from a so-called society publication to become a broad-ranging periodical, which not only encourages a talent for living, but deals with significant contemporary issues, a publication edited for the af-

fluent reader who is literate, cultured and socially conscious. His leadership has increased circulation from 100,000 in 1972 to over 400,000 readers today.

During his career, he has edited more than 45,000 pages of magazines and has had an extraordinary record in discovering and developing new and original graphic talents. Frank Zachary is not only the father of a whole generation of creative magazine art directors and photographers but an inspiration to artist and designers throughout the world. He is a beloved legend still excited with ideas and plans.

8

PRESIDENTIAL SWEEPSTAKES
## GEORGE BUSH

THE VICE PRESIDENT RODE
TO THE TOP WITH
RONALD REAGAN. WILL HE NOW
FOLLOW HIM DOWN?

BY JAMES HORWITZ

PRESIDENTIAL SWEEPSTAKES
## MICHAEL DUKAKIS

WITH HIS STERN
GREEK SOUL, THE GOVERNOR
IS READY TO SPOON OUT
SOME STRONG MEDICINE

BY A. CRAIG COPETAS

PRESIDENTIAL SWEEPSTAKES
## PIERRE DU PONT

BEFORE HE CAN WEAR
THE CROWN OF THE PRESIDENCY,
HE'S GOT TO OVERCOME
THE CURSE OF OLD MONEY

BY NELSON W. ALDRICH, JR.

PRESIDENTIAL SWEEPSTAKES
## RICHARD GEPHARDT

THE CONGRESSMAN IS AS
WHOLESOME AS A HEARTLAND
SUMMER—AN ANOMALY
IN A COLD, CRUEL WORLD

BY RON DORFMAN

PRESIDENTIAL SWEEPSTAKES
## ALBERT GORE

THE SENATOR'S ROOTS
MAY BE ON A TENNESSEE FARM,
BUT AT HEART HE'S
A WASHINGTON ANIMAL.

BY GARRETT EPPS

PRESIDENTIAL SWEEPSTAKES
## MARIO CUOMO

NEW YORK'S GOVERNOR IS
HAPPIEST WHEN HE'S MISERABLE,
AND HE KNOWS THE PRESIDENCY
WOULD BE PURE AGONY

BY JACK NEWFIELD

10

Publication **Regardie's**
Art Directors **Rip Georges, Pamela Berry**
Designers **Rip Georges, Pamela Berry**
Illustrators **J. Wooley, J. Bennett, S. Pietsch, R. Hess,**
**S. McCray, D. Maffia, C.F. Payne, A. Kunz, S. Earley, A. Russo,**
**S. Brodner, M. Arisman**
Publisher **Regardie's**
Category **Special Section and Illustration**
Date **November / December 1987**

## PRESIDENTIAL SWEEPSTAKES

# ROBERT
# DOLE

"BEING THE MOST intelligent member of the Senate, he'll be the most cynical," says Fred Whitehead, one of the few prairie populists left in the overwhelmingly Republican state of Kansas. Bob Dole's Kansas. A state where Dole's most recent opponent considered the effort so futile that he spent $1,000, printed no literature, and received only 29 percent of the vote.

Whitehead is talking about one of Dole's more famous punch lines—"See no evil, hear no evil, and evil"—which refers, respectively, to former presidents Carter, Ford, and Nixon. If you think about it, a lot of Dole's one-liners contain disabled chagrin and honesty, intelligence and cynicism, charm and vindictiveness. But what are the essential dualities of the man himself? Mr. Small Town, U.S.A.? Mr. Washington insider? Mr. Married Man? Mr. Divorce? Mr. Self-reliant? Mr. Compassion? Mr. Moderate Republican? Mr. Conservative Republican? How many pairs of abstractions does it take to add up to one concrete Kansas senator who wants to be president? And what elements of character connect any two halves of Robert Dole? What is the body? And what is the soul?

"My impression," says Ed Rube, a professor at the University of Kansas, "is that he's a Republican, Dole's an honest man."

Rube is an old-line New Deal liberal with an affection for Robert Nixon and his career. He was once cured of a stomach ailment with the Watergate

|  |
|---|
| IT'S EASY TO LIKE |
| THE MAN, BUT |
| IT'S HARD TO FIGURE |
| HIS POLITICS |
| BY ROBERT DAY |

proceedings. "The nurses would bring me the *New York Times* in the morning," he says, "and the more I read, the better I felt. By the afternoon I didn't have to take my pills. By the time Nixon resigned I was well."

Whitehead, Rube, and I are in Kansas City. I've reread what we came to call, in memory of the Checkers speech, a "Republican Oldsmobile"—a huge 1-51 of a car complete with cruise control and hello that ring when you leave the turn signal on for too long or the gas gets too low. It's a geriatric special, a combination of 1970s American bulk and 1980s Eurotrash styles. We've punched in a temperature and a speed, and we're taking Interstate 70 into the sun 250 miles west toward Russell, Kansas—"Bob Dole country." Ahead of us is a line of Kansas towns flattened up against the interstate. Lawrence. Topeka. Junction City. Abilene. Salina. Russell. Hays. Wa Keeney. Our idea is to do a little Republican bashing and to talk about Dole and what he might be like as president. Considering who's in the Oldsmobile. Barbed-wire Bob fares pretty well. In

fact, two days later, coming back down the same road, we're worried about how well he fares.

KANSAS SEEMS SO vacant to the rest of the United States (and to much of its more prominent citizens have become a matter of love. Larry Nature. All London. Rayer Keaton. Matt Dillon. Doc Brinkley (you never heard of Doc Brinkley, the pioneer of the goat testicle transplant?). Amelia Earhart. Wyatt Earp. Dwight Eisenhower. Gary Hart. On the Kansas turnpike, the three of us talk about Dole's regard for the underdog and the outcast. We conclude that it's probably a result of his own disability. We picture him in his typical pose, his left shoulder thrust slightly forward, some document or book in his left hand, as if it might draw one's attention from what he can not hold in his other hand. His eyes look upward and away. We cannot see his right hand, the extremity with which other politicians grasp the hands of voters.

Dole returned home to Russell to practice law because it was the only place he could feel comfortable with his injury.

"He didn't have to explain it to us," says Dean Banker of Banker's Department Store. "We were just proud he was alive."

Out of our left window is Lawrence and the University of Kansas, where Dole was once a student and a first athlete and where Whitehead and I attended school. Out of right lies the football stadium. We

DAN McCOY

## PRESIDENTIAL SWEEPSTAKES

# HOWARD
# BAKER

DO YOU BELIEVE in miracles? You just about have to if you want Howard Baker to be the nation's next president. Baker isn't running. Not so long ago someone who wasn't running could still be nominated and even elected. Nowadays, however, if you want to be president, you have to go out there and grovel like everybody else.

This is something that Baker isn't doing and isn't going to do. When Baker decided to succeed Donald Regan as President Reagan's chief of staff, he knew he was giving up his presidential ambitions for 1988. He understands himself and his situation, perhaps with fewer illusions than most politicians. His hobby, after all, is photography. Almost anywhere he goes, on official business or not, he carries a camera. A photographer is an observer, both of the world around him and of himself. A good photographer—and Baker is considered to be good for an amateur—observes with a minimum of illusions. This is a good trait to have in a president, but a bad one for someone who has to have a vision and persuade others that it will come to pass.

It's important to remember that public people are private people, too. Public people have as many scars and weaknesses as the rest of us, and Baker isn't unfamiliar with struggles and sorrows. He mother died when he was eight. His former marriage of three years later, and Baker, like so many other children who found themselves in similar situations, resented the new woman in his father's life.

Baker's adult years weren't free of pain either. His wife, the former Joy Dirksen, the

|  |
|---|
| THE CHIEF OF STAFF |
| HAS ONLY ONE CARD LEFT TO |
| PLAY, AND IT'S GOING TO TAKE |
| A FEW CARDS TO |
| TRUMP IT |
| BY JON MARGOLIS |

daughter of the late, legendary Senator Everett Dirksen of Illinois, was one of the first well-known women in the country to go public about having a drinking problem.

All of which is enough to make a fellow doubt whether being the most powerful man in the world is the most important thing in the world. And that may explain why a few months ago, before Baker accepted his White House appointment, a visitor got the distinct impression that he wouldn't go for the nomination. It wasn't anything he said. On the contrary, most of what he said made him sound like someone who was about to get in there and mix it up. No, it was because he acted as if he was content with his life. He seems to enjoy having the perks of power as much as he enjoys not having the pressures that accompany them. He likes being important enough to have powerful people seek his advice as much as he likes not having to make major decisions every day. Again, perhaps such a man should be president. But such a man rarely gets to be president.

On the other hand, Baker did run (rather poorly) for president once in 1980, and he gave up his Senate seat in 1984 so that he could try again in 1988. In other words,

he has had occasional bouts of presidentialitis, a disease whose which fellow sufferer Morris Udall once remarked, "There is only one known cure for this exhilarating fluid."

If the miracle does happen and Baker is nominated, he'd have an excellent chance of winning the general election. Although nothing in politics is certain, one very good bet is that Baker is the most electable of all Republicans. He isn't saddled with George Bush's image as a permanent second banana. Robert Dole's occasional meanness or Jack Kemp's ideological rigidity. Furthermore, one could make a reasonably strong case that he'd make a very good president. Baker, as much as anyone around, understands government, knows how to get things done, and is prudent but not easily pushed around.

Most of the politicians who would love to see Baker run have already endorsed someone else, so they aren't repeating their support for Baker on the record. Even Baker's biggest booster, Senator Warren Rudman of New Hampshire, is going to support Senator Robert Dole. But when asked whether Rudman and his associates still harbor secret hopes that Baker will somehow get nominated, a senior official in Dole's campaign replied, "There's absolutely no doubt about it." "But," he did the president is...

DANIEL MAFFIA

## PRESIDENTIAL SWEEPSTAKES

# BRUCE
# BABBITT

IT WAS SPIT-AND-WHITTLE time, that time in early afternoon August—on central Iowa when the heat presses on the earth and squeezes out energy, when farmers idle in the shade near their carpets of corn like trout lying nose-to-current on a streambed. But the day's schedule for Bruce Babbitt, the former governor of Arizona and a candidate for the presidency, called for him to make six speeches, so he was bouncing around rural, dying farm, grocery-calendar Jesus, hog and hominy country seeking support. You have to court the spoiled Iowans. Every one of them expects to meet and look you over personally, as a bull does a new gate.

Twenty of them waited for Babbitt in the back room of Polly's Restaurant in Parkersburg, one of the area's many small towns that seem unchanged from 100 years ago, when church-walkers used to wake chrome sweaters by poking them with sticks tipped with squirrels' tails. Babbitt, a lanky column of a man dressed in his usual immaculate Boston-banker black suit, entered and began to shake hands. "It all, sincere, intellectual niceness without any public speaking ability," is how his wife, Hattie, described him 11 years ago, at the beginning of his successful campaign to become Arizona's attorney general.

Not only does Babbitt look the same at 49, he still has the air of a philosopher-intraining. Instead of the usual politician's convivial backs; warmth that quickly leaves shyness, Babbitt is reserved and controlled. It's a highly polished surface that he slaves on and is careful not to scratch. Like Canada, he gives respect but fires no toxicity.

|  |
|---|
| HE'S CREATIVE, |
| SMART, AND WITTY— |
| AND BOY, DOES HE |
| HAVE A LONG WAY TO GO |
| BY RICHARD WEST |

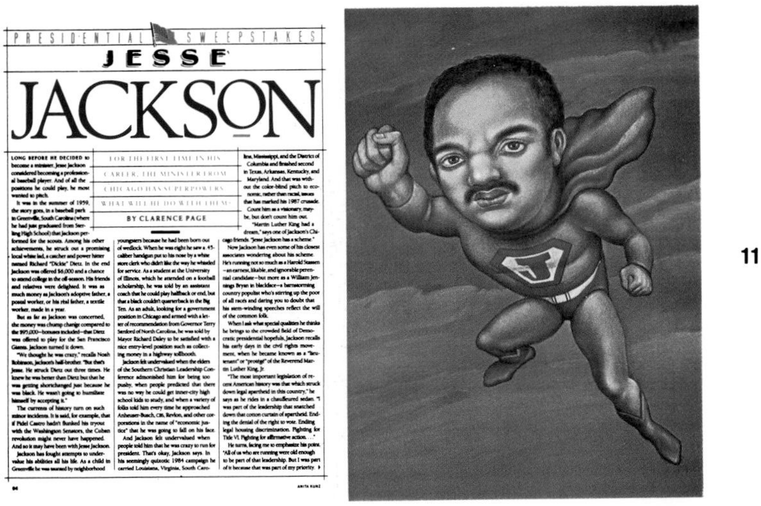

Whatever else Babbitt makes of his personality will always be peripheral. His real strength is his far-reaching and acute intellect. He loves ideas and government's inner workings as much as Gary Hart loves young women who pour over him only for Hart has to pander. And if he isn't exactly a picklemeister orator, at least his starched cuff prose doesn't always sound like an editorial, as it once did. Nowadays he things to remind Mr. Chips reciting an erudite essay.

For the third time since startup Babbitt began the same speech, a brief biography that covers his decision to enter public life after he saw "the face of starvation" while he worked as a geologist in South America, his joining Marriott Luther King in civil rights marches in Alabama while he studied law at Harvard, and his successful political career as a moderate Democrat in the conservative Republican state of Arizona. When Babbitt applying the lash to the Reagan administration's farm policy and trade practices as well as to Meander or the Iceland summit, Babbitt worked up some real homespun 19th-century muckracking indignation over its foreign policy, which he apparently thinks was designed by Shirley MacLaine. Though he's no joke teller, he got a liberty

laugh with his line. "If the Iran-gate committees had looked a little deeper, they would have found a connection between Reagan and the presidency."

Finally Babbitt came to what amounted to the bedrock of his candidacy. After eight years of "government by Teleflopping Tent," he believes that America can't want a brainy leader with his head just graduated from Sterling High School's that Jackson performed for the nation. Among his other achievements, he struck out a promising local white bid, a teacher and prowar lover named Richard "Dickie" Dara. In the end Jackson was offered $6,000 and a chance to attend college in the off-season. His friends and relatives were delighted. It was so much money as Jackson's adoptive father, a postal worker, or his old father, a textile worker, made in a year.

But as far as Jackson was concerned, the money was chump change compared to the $95,000+ bonuses included—that Dara was offered to play for the San Francisco Giants. Jackson turned it down.

"We thought he was crazy," recalls Noah Robinson, Jackson's half-brother. "But that's Jesse. He struck Dara out three times. He knew he was better than Dara but that he was getting short-changed just because he was black. He wasn't going to humiliate himself by accepting it."

The currents of history turn on such minor incidents. It is said, for example, that if Fidel Castro hadn't fumbled his tryout with the Washington Senators, the Cuban revolution might never have happened. And so it may have been with Jesse Jackson. Jackson has fought attempts to undervalue his abilities all his life. As a child in Greenville he was treated by neighborhood

C. F. PAYNE

## PRESIDENTIAL SWEEPSTAKES

# JESSE
# JACKSON

LONG BEFORE HE DECIDED to become a minister, Jesse Jackson considered becoming a professional baseball player. And of all the positions he could play, he most wanted to pitch.

It was in the summer of 1959, the story goes, in a baseball park in Greenville, South Carolina (where he had just graduated from Sterling High School) that Jackson performed for the nation. Among his other achievements, he struck out a promising local white kid, a teacher and power hitter named Richard "Dickie" Dara. In the end Jackson was offered $6,000 and a chance to attend college in the off-season. His friends and relatives were delighted. It was so much money as Jackson's adoptive father, a postal worker, or his old father, a textile worker, made in a year.

But as far as Jackson was concerned, the money was chump change compared to the $95,000+ bonuses included—that Dara was offered to play for the San Francisco Giants. Jackson turned it down.

"We thought he was crazy," recalls Noah Robinson, Jackson's half-brother. "But that's Jesse. He struck Dara out three times. He knew he was better than Dara but that he was getting short-changed just because he was black. He wasn't going to humiliate himself by accepting it."

The currents of history turn on such minor incidents. It is said, for example, that if Fidel Castro hadn't fumbled his tryout with the Washington Senators, the Cuban revolution might never have happened. And so it may have been with Jesse Jackson. Jackson has fought attempts to undervalue his abilities all his life. As a child in Greenville he was treated by neighborhood

|  |
|---|
| FOR THE FIRST TIME IN HIS |
| CAREER, THE MINISTER FROM |
| OHIO AGITHAS AN PERFORMS |
| WHAT WILL HE DO WITH CLOUT? |
| BY CLARENCE PAGE |

line, Mississippi, and the District of Columbia and finished second in Texas, Arkansas, Kentucky, and Maryland. And that was without the color-blind pinch to economic name, rather than racial, issues that has marched his 1987 crusade. Count him as a visionary, maybe but not...

Warren Luther King had a dream," says one of Jackson's Chicago friends. "Jesse Jackson has a scheme."

Now Jackson has even some of his clients associates wondering about his scheme. He's running not so much as a Harold Stassen—an eternity, likable, and ignorable perennial candidate—but more as a William Jennings Bryan in blackface—a barnstorming country populist who's stirring up the poor of all races and daring you to doubt that his seen-winding speeches reflect the will of the common folk.

When I ask what special qualities he thinks he brings to the crowded field of Democratic presidential hopefuls, Jackson recalls his early days in the civil rights movement. Here, where he became known as a "lieutenant" or "protégé" of the Reverend Martin Luther King, Jr.

"The most important legislation of recent American history was that which struck down legal apartheid in this country," he says as he rides in a chauffeured sedan. "A vast part of the leadership that marched down that common current of apartheid. Ending the denial of the right to vote. Ending legal housing discrimination. Fighting for Title VI fighting for affirmative action. . ."

He turns, locking me to emphasize his point. "All of us who are running were old enough to be part of that leadership. But I was part of it because that was part of my priority. I

ANITA KUNZ

## PRESIDENTIAL SWEEPSTAKES

# PAT
# ROBERTSON

BRACE YOURSELVES, FOLKS! The roaring 20th century is boiling up to a climax! In the next 12 years MILLENNIAL MADNESS is gonna inundate this planet!

Check out the history books and read about the years 987 to 1000. In those days a lot of fruit loops were running around and stirring up trouble. Exactly 1,000 years ago Grand Prince Vladimir of Russia started a religious cold war by joining the Eastern Orthodox Catholic Church. The Persians and Arabs and Christians were waging a holy war. People were scared and confused back then—just as they are today.

And in the next 12 years, I believe we will see similar irrational kookiness, messianic megalomaniacs, mass insanities, apocalyptic paroxysms, end-of-world prophecies, demented demagogues, holy wars, crazy crusades, lunatic leaders, dishearten demagogues, and thousands of just plain old fourscore-square evangelical bad trips. Ollie North. Jim Bakker. Gary Hart. Muammar Qaddafi. Shirley MacLaine. the Ayatollah Khomeini. Oral Roberts, and yes, Pat Robertson—they're just warm-ups for the eccentricities and terror-activated manias to come.

No question about it, most of the violence and angry politics that are apparent these days pit one biblical god against another. The Cold War has taken a backseat. It's as if America and Russia have become mere pawns on God's chessboard. It's the roaring 9th century all over again! Feudal Super Bowl crusader time! My God vs. your Great Satan! Israel vs. Rome vs. Byzantium. Shiites vs. Sunnis. Hindus vs. Buddhists. Hindus vs. Sikhs. Jehovah vs. Allah for the world championship.

And now, with the emergence of the mili-

|  |
|---|
| IS HE MERELY A |
| FINE-TUNED TELEVISION |
| EVANGELIST, OR DID |
| THE AMERICAN ANATOLIAN |
| BY TIMOTHY LEARY |

tant Evangelicals and the candidacy of Reverend Pat Robertson, the angry, jealous, fundamentalist God has thrown his bellicose hat into the American political ring.

I have studied the skillfully written press releases of the Christian Broadcasting Network, a monstrously successful media empire that had a sales of $180 million last year. I have pored over stacks of lavishly adulatory columns on Robertson from smalltown newspapers and unashamedly adoring articles in mainline publications I was stunned, for example, to read this Chicago *Tribune* headline: THE 670 MIRACLE NAMED GBN. It was subtitled "With the Lord's Grace, Pat Robertson builds a Cable Empire."

Huh? A presumably rational newspaper involves the Deity in the discussion of a political candidate?

What is the world coming to?

ROBERTSON'S PLATFORM isn't all that surprising. It's your standard right-wing, strident, millenarian kook show: Predestination, here we come. The familiar Jimmy Swaggart, Oral Roberts, Pat Buchanan, Ronnie Reagan platform. An appeal to the chosen people. An expectation of the investment and miraculous intervention of God or his messianic prophet. A belief in the total transformation to the perfect kingdom. An eternal struggle against the Evil Empire.

Fiercely ascetic white-bread puritanism. Armageddonian antigun witch-hunting. Pro-school prayer, pro-creationist "science." What astonishes and disturbs me, however, is the charismatic power of Robertson's evangelical tv show. The "700 Club" is designed to produce an altered state of consciousness, a classic voodoo hypnotic trance.

To begin with, the show's production is that of state-of-the-art prime-time TV—it uses the same slick, commercial techniques that seduce us into buying Coors beer and Extra-Strength Tylenol. The actors who appear on the show look like local news anchors. Dignified Ben Kinchlow with his white-trimmed mustache he looks like a Supreme Court justice. The lovely assistant, Danuta Soderman, looks like a model for some sensible home product such as Drano or Ranch Motel.

The program builds efficiently toward its climax, namely the invocation of the Deity. Buckle your seat belts, trippers, while Shaman Pat leans over, his eyes clenched in pain-felt concentration. Hey, the guy's possessed! Then, when the audience is whipped into a classic trance-state and neurologically vulnerable, Robertson starts to imprint the commercials. He slides up the sponsor and starts to discuss God's agenda—namely His impatience with what's happening on the planet. Both Robertson and the Almighty Lord are "sick and tired" (the candidate's favorite buzz phrase) of God's cruelty being taken over by sinners, homosexuals, Democrats, secular humanists, atheist scientists, communist dupes, pornographers, and, above all, the anti-Christ humanist. Meanwhile the older pious-looking chap next to Robertson—the guy who's waiting for the word.

SEAN EARLEY

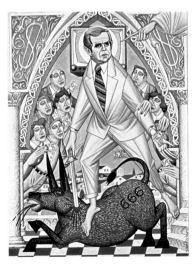

## PRESIDENTIAL SWEEPSTAKES

# PAUL
# SIMON

AS PAUL SIMON got off the plane, the cops were waiting for him.

For many Illinois politicians, such a sight would provoke a quick retreat down the jetway—or at least a demand to speak to an attorney. But for Paul Simon, the perpetual Democratic U.S. senator from the state and a presidential candidate, it meant only that he was getting better treatment than he thought he better deserved.

In fact, Simon's campaign has in common with most other politicians. When he was eight he's—of life—wanted to be a newspaperman, and by the time he was 19 he had bought a weekly newspaper in Troy, Illinois. It was also a state where political corruption is almost a badge of immaturity among politicians, where two of the last four elected governors have been felons.

But Illinois is where Simon has built a reputation that is not only clean but pristine. I am not sure whether he can tie a half hitch or a sheepshank, but in all other respects, Paul Simon is America's Boy Scout. "No like," a friend says, "is a Frank Capra movie."

But Mr. Simon has already gone to Washington. Now he wants to move into the White House.

As O'Hare, Chicago patrolman Don Graham brings up the rear just in case any-body wants to get near enough to actually speak to Simon, something the candidate would welcome. Grasnew leans over to Bernie-ta'lscheersen, the sole Simon aide who has met him here at the airport. "Next time call," he tells her. "We pick him up right at the plane in a patrol car. Take you wherever you want. Simple."

|  |
|---|
| THE SUN SHINES IN A CAMPAIGN |
| CONSULTANT'S NIGHTMARE— |
| BUT THIS APPEAL ECHOES THE HEART |
| OF THE AMERICAN DREAM |
| BY ROGER SIMON |

Talkmann seems stunned that anybody, let alone Paul Simon, could have such a thing arranged for him. "You would?" she says. "You actually would?"

"Hey," Grasney says, "that is what we do."

But, alas, it is not what Paul Simon does. And he will accept no police escort as he prepares to set off into murderous traffic. It's talky mankind jeep for the trek to suburban Park Ridge, where he will catch a commuter flight to Springfield. Patrolman Kovac helps Simon load his luggage into the back of the jeep. "Hey get the right guy in the White House," he says to Simon, "and maybe I'll see the inside of the place." The rage of it is true that always working the angles.

In the front seat of the car, Simon sets immediately to work. He calls a Boston radio show using the briefcase telephone in the backseat. The radio station has taken a poll and Simon has done "surprisingly" well, though he isn't told what that means.

The interviewer only one side of which I can hear—begins typically: "I'm still wearing the smaller ones," Simon (who is no relation to me) says, "not the big butterfly ones." He is talking about his bow tie, his trademark, which appears on his bumper stickers and buttons, and a small silver medal of which can be purchased at his campaign events for $5.

The bow tie, which he simply happens to like, has become more than a trademark, however. It helps sum up the Simon strategy, the Simon message. We are different in a race where nearly everyone else is alike. I

ANTHONY RUSSO

11

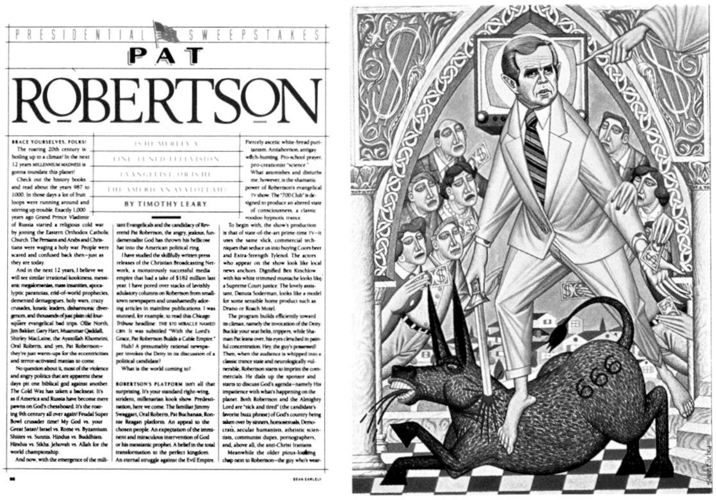

Publication **Art Center Review #2**
Art Director **Kit Hinrichs**
Designers **Kit Hinrichs, Lenore Gartz**
Illustrators **John Mattos, Walid Saba**
Photographers **Henrik Kam, Steven Hellor**
Client **Art Center College of Design**
Agency **Pentagram Design**
Category **Single Issue**
Date **October 1, 1987**

12

Publication **Photo Metro**
Art Director **Henry Brimmer**
Photographer **Charly Franklin**
Publisher **Photo Metro**
Category **Single Issue**
Date **September 1987**

Publication **Premiere**
Art Directors **David Walters, Robert Best**
Designers **Robert Best, David Walters**
Publisher **Murdoch / Hachette**
Category **New Magazine**
Date **October 1987**

## A Daughter's
# REVENGE

# A DECADE ON THE SET WITH
# WOODY ALLEN

PHOTOGRAPHED BY
**Brian Hamill**

# THE
# SURE THING

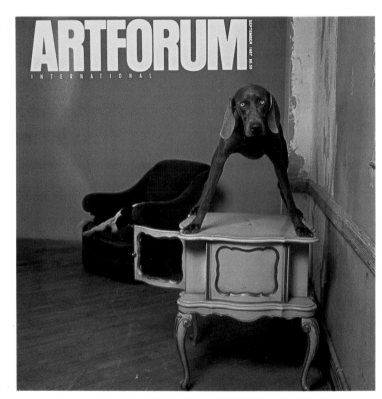

Publication **The Boston Globe Magazine**
Art Director **Lucy Bartholomay**
Designer **Lucy Bartholomay**
Publisher **Boston Globe**
Category **Cover**
Date **July 1987**

Publication **Artforum**
Art Director **Tibor Kalman**
Designer **Emily Oberman**
Photographer **William Wegman**
Photo Editor **Melissa Harris**
Client **Artforum**
Agency **M & Co.**
Category **Cover**
Date **September 1987**

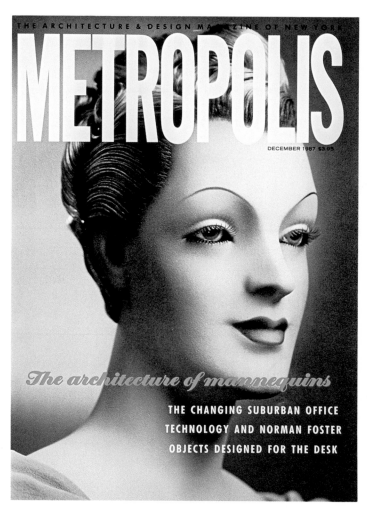

16

Publication **The Wall Street Journal**
Art Director **Joe Dizney**
Designer **Joe Dizney**
Illustrator **David Suter**
Publisher **Dow Jones & Company, Inc.**
Category **Cover**
Date **September 18, 1987**

Publication **Metropolis**
Art Director **Helene Silverman**
Designer **Helene Silverman**
Publisher **Metropolis Magazine**
Category **Cover**
Date **December 1987**

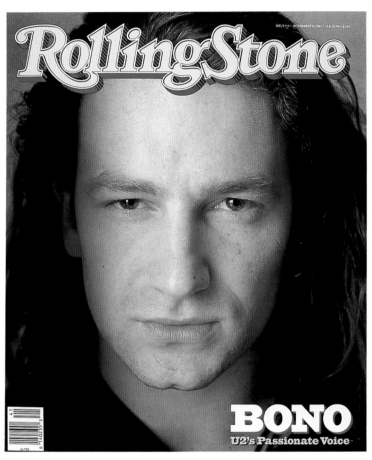

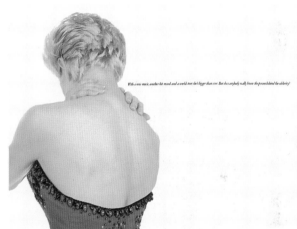

Publication **Rolling Stone**

Art Director **Fred Woodward**

Designer **Fred Woodward**

Photographer **Matthew Rolston**

Photo Editor **Laurie Kratochvil**

Publisher **Straight Arrow Publishers**

Category **Cover**

Date **October 8, 1987**

Publication **Rolling Stone**

Art Director **Fred Woodward**

Designer **Fred Woodward**

Photographer **Herb Ritts**

Photo Editor **Laurie Kratochvil**

Publisher **Straight Arrow Publishers**

Category **Single Page / Spread**

Date **September 10, 1987**

Publication **Frankfurter Allgemeine Magazin**
Art Director **Hans Georg Pospischill**
Designer **Seymour Chwast**
Illustrator **Seymour Chwast**
Agency **The Pushpin Group**
Category **Story Presentation**
Date **December 4, 1987**

18

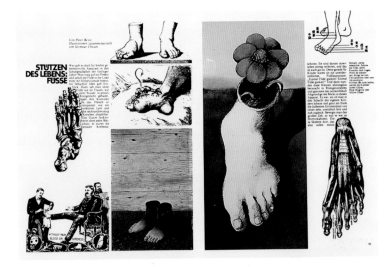

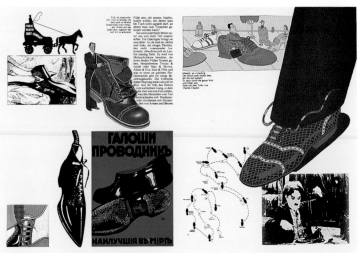

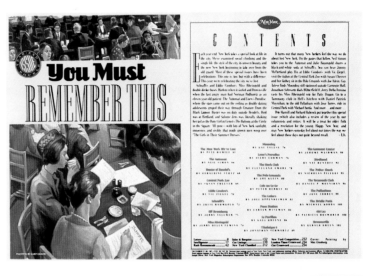

19

Publication **New York**
Art Director **Robert Best**
Designer **Josh Gosfield**
Illustrator **Max Ginsburg**
Publisher **News Group America**
Category **Single Issue**
Date **December 21-28, 1987**

Publication **The New York Times Magazine**
Art Director **Diana LaGuardia**
Designer **Audrone Razgaitis**
Photographer **Various**
Publisher **The New York Times**
Category **Story Presentation**
Date **February 1, 1987**

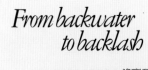

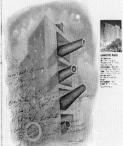

Publication **The Boston Globe Magazine**
Art Director **Lucy Bartholomay**
Designer **Lucy Bartholomay**
Illustrators **Lane Smith, Marc Rosenthal, Andrezj Dudzinski,**
**Blair Thornley**
Publisher **The Boston Globe**
Category **Story Presentation**
Date **September 6, 1987**

Publication **Spy**
Art Director **Alexander Isley**
Designer **Alexander Isley**
Illustrator **George Stubbs**
Photographer **Frederick Lewis**
Photo Editor **Amy Stark**
Publisher **Spy Publishing Partners**
Category **Single Page / Spread**
Date **August 1987**

What ever happened to Mary Jo Kopechne's five girlfriends who had the good fortune *not* to drive off with Ted Kennedy? See page 37. Why has there never been a best-seller or a movie or even a television docudrama about Chappaquiddick? See page 40. In the age of Everythingscam and Whatevergate, how, after 18 years, can the Chappaquiddick cover-up remain so airtight? Good question. And why won't anybody publish an impressive new investigative book that for once gets a Kennedy cousin and Chappaquiddick witness *on the record* about the incident? Read this article.

E ARLY IN THE MORNING of July 19, 1969, after attending an intimate party of male political cronies and female political aides, Senator Edward Kennedy drove his Oldsmobile off Chappaquiddick Island's Dyke Bridge and into Poucha Pond. His passenger, Mary Jo Kopechne, drowned.

# CHAPPAQUIDDICK

*The Unsold Story*

BY TAD FRIEND

TRANSLUCENT

Publication **Spy**
Art Director **Alexander Isley**
Designer **Alexander Isley**
Illustrator **Alexander Isley**
Publisher **Spy Publishing Partners**
Category **Single Page / Spread**
Date **November 1987**

Publication **Accessories**
Art Director **Hans Gschliesser**
Designer **Hans Gschliesser**
Photographer **Stephen Huszar**
Photo Editor **Hans Gschliesser**
Publisher **Business Journals, Inc.**
Category **Single Page / Spread**
Date **February 1, 1988**

Publication **Simpson Paper—The Annual Report Client**
Art Director **Bennett Robinson**
Illustrator **Skip Liepke**
Client **Simpson Paper Company**
Agency **Corporate Graphics, Inc.**
Category **Single Issue**
Date **October 1987**

THE ANNUAL REPORT CLIENT

DAVID BITHER FOR WARNER COMMUNICATIONS

**NORTHROP**

LES DALY FOR NORTHROP CORPORATION

SAM YANES FOR POLAROID CORPORATION

JIM SWEENEY FOR CAREMARK, INC.

TIM CARR FOR DOMINO'S PIZZA, INC.

TOM McINTOSH FOR H. J. HEINZ COMPANY

JESS HAY FOR LOMAS & NETTLETON

**Reebok**

SHARON COHEN FOR REEBOK INTERNATIONAL LTD

PUBLICATION
DESIGN ANNUAL
SILVER

EQUITABLE INVESTMENT CORPORATION

A REVIEW OF THE
INVESTMENT SUBSIDIARIES

1986

**23**

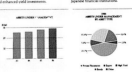

Publication **EIC Annual Report**
Art Director **Paul Waner**
Designer **Gary Lew**
Photographer **Michael Heintz**
Photo Editor **Paul Waner**
Client **Equitable Investment Corporation**
Agency **Donaldson, Lufkin & Jenrette**
Category **Single Issue**
Date **May 15, 1987**

Publication **Potlatch Annual Report**
Art Director **Kit Hinrichs**
Designers **Kit Hinrichs, Lenore Bartz**
Photographers **Tom Tracey, Paul Fusco, Gerald Bybee**
Client **Potlatch Corporation**
Agency **Pentagram Design**
Category **Single Issue**
Date **March 1, 1987**

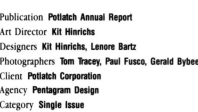

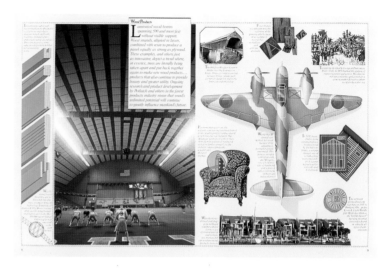

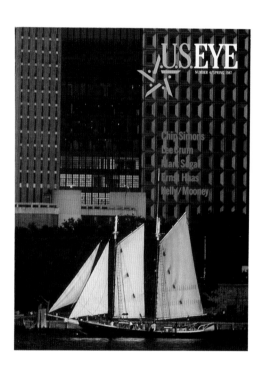

Publication **U.S. Eye**
Art Director **Anthony Russell**
Designer **Casey Clark**
Photographers **Chip Simons, Lee Crum, Mark Segal,**
**Ernst Haas, Kelly/Mooney**
Client **Anthony Russell, Inc.**
Agency **Anthony Russell, Inc.**
Category **Single Issue**
Date **Spring 1987**

Publication **Art Center Review #1**
Art Director **Kit Hinrichs**
Designers **Kit Hinrichs, Lenore Bartz**
Illustrators **John Hersey, John Mattos**
Photographer **Henrik Kam**
Client **Art Center College of Design**
Agency **Pentagram Design**
Category **Single Issue**
Date **May 1, 1987**

Publication **Industry Update '87**
Art Director **Terry Ross Koppel**
Designer **Terry Ross Koppel**
Client **Queens Group**
Agency **Koppel & Scher**
Category **Special Section**
Date **May 1987**

Publication **Spy**
Art Director **Alexander Isley**
Designers **Alexander Isley, Catherine Gilmore-Barnes,**
**Alexander Knowlton**
Photo Editor **Amy Stark**
Publisher **Spy Publishing Partners**
Category **Overall**
Date **July, August, November, December 1987**

What ever happened to Mary Jo Kopechne's five girlfriends who had the good fortune *not* to drive off with Ted Kennedy? See page 37. Why has there never been a best-seller or a movie or even a television docudrama about Chappaquiddick? See page 40. In the age of Everythingscam and Whatevergate, how, after 18 years, can the Chappaquiddick cover-up remain so airtight? Good question. And why won't anybody publish an impressive new investigative book that for once gets a Kennedy cousin and Chappaquiddick witness *on the record* about the incident? Read this article

EARLY IN THE MORNING of July 19, 1969, after attending an intimate party of male political cronies and female political aides, Senator Edward Kennedy drove his Oldsmobile off Chappaquiddick Island's Dyke Bridge and into Poucha Pond. His passenger, Mary Jo Kopechne, drowned.

This is not exactly news. Most of us recall that after a considerable public rumpus, Senator Kennedy took the extraordinary step of going on television to explain—although exactly what he explained unconvincingly—this latest Kennedy tragedy.

Kennedy pleaded guilty to leaving the scene of an accident after causing personal injury and later promised to consider resigning his Senate seat (blah blah, he evidently decided, instead going on to win reelection three times).

# CHAPPAQUIDDICK

## The Unsold Story

BY TAD FRIEND

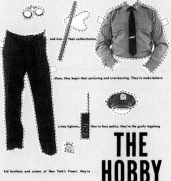

**19:42 HOURS** (or thereabouts), June 17. Officer Robin Riccio, in civilian garb, is brushing away the crumbs at Officer Nick Diomede, a genuine police officer, polishes off the last of his sandwich...

# THE HOBBY COPS

BY JAMES TRAUB
PHOTOGRAPHS BY ED GABEL

SPY has always been troubled by the very real discrimination faced by women with enormous breasts, the leering glances, the stereotyping by chest-obsessed males, harassment in the workplace. Thus, the remarkable undercover investigation that follows—an article conceived, written and edited by women. It is presented not to titillate our readers, or because we thought that mentioning it on the cover would sell more copies of the magazine. No. We did it because, as journalists, we have a sacred mandate to expose social injustice no matter how sensational. And so, in the ground-breaking tradition of *Black Like Me* and *Gentleman's Agreement*, for two weeks so she could personally experience the shame, the burden—and, yes, the undeniable retro glamour of being

**FOR YEARS,** the idea had intrigued me, and tantalized me, and the day I saw Phil Donahue interview a panel of women about their breasts, it returned more insistently than ever. *If a small-busted woman were to become a large-busted woman, I wondered, what adjustments would she have to make?*

# BUSTY LIKE *me*

"The only way to bridge the gap was to become temporarily bosomy really bosomy. For two weeks I did everything I normally did, wore everything I normally wore. The only difference was in the Size of My Breasts"

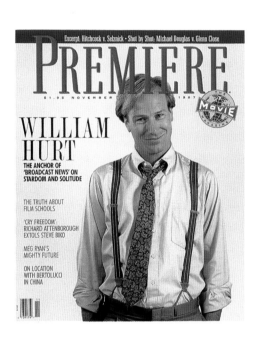

Publication **Premiere**
Art Directors **David Walters, Robert Best**
Designers **Robert Best, David Walters**
Photographer **Various**
Publisher **Murdoch / Hachette**
Category **Overall**
Date **October, November, December 1987**

Publication **Pacific**
Art Director **Michael Mabry**
Designers **Michael Mabry, Piper Murakami, Renee Holson**
Photo Editor **Teresa Ruano**
Client **Pacific Telesis**
Agency **Michael Mabry Design, Inc.**
Category **Overall**
Date **August, September, October 1987**

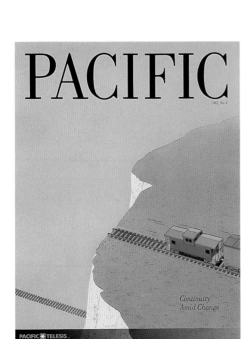

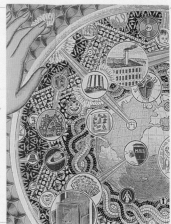

31

Publication **San Francisco Focus**
Art Director **Matthew Drace**
Designer **Mark Ulriksen**
Publisher **Doug Salin**
Publisher **KQED**
Category **Redesign**
Date **November 1, 1987**

Publication **Architectural Record**
Art Director **Alberto Bucchianeri**
Designers **Alberto Bucchianeri, Anna Egger-Schlesinger**
Publisher **McGraw-Hill, Inc.**
Category **Overall**
Date **June 1987**

## Bastion of culture

*Amid political unrest, the South Korean government has unveiled its first major monument, a museum of modern art that reflects a continuing cultural duality.*

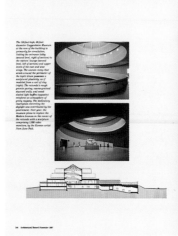

Publication **The New York Times / Arts & Leisure**
Art Directors **Linda Brewer, Tom Bodkin**
Designer **Tom Bodkin**
Publisher **The New York Times**
Category **Redesign**
Date **March 8, 1987**

Publication **Conde Nast's Traveler**
Art Director **Lloyd Ziff**
Designer **Lloyd Ziff**
Photographer **Helmut Newton**
Photo Editor **Kathleen Klech**
Publisher **Conde Nast Publications, Inc.**
Category **Story Presentation**
Date **October 1987**

Field notes
When it's your hometown you know a few places that others might miss

The discreet face of Das Exil

# Berlin
# by Helmut Newton

Dear Traveler,
This report is certainly not by an innocent in Berlin. 2 items take precedence over everything else: Food and women. Of course, ambience counts for a lot, too. I guess that the majority of the places I visited would not be the kind of addresses given by the concierge at the Kempinski or the InterContinental. After all, this is my hometown.

I stayed at the Askanischer Hof--very central--on the Kurfürstendamm, always referred to as the Ku'damm. I had one of the 2 suites available there. Mine, facing out back, very quiet, the only thing that rudely wakes you in the early a.m. are very aggressively yelling Berlin birds. My suite had a sitting room and bedroom, large. The breakfast incl. in the price is so copious that you don't need a big lunch, and the whole costs you DM 220 for 2. The furniture is Berlin style 1940s, and it sure is quaint. Downstairs there is a cafe called the Tasty, referred to by some of my friends as the Lebenslänglich, i.e., the lifelong, as apparently many of its patrons have been long-term inmates of the local prisons.
The beer garden where I photographed the 2 blond women with their friends is well worth a visit: It's a 25 min. drive from Ku'damm, it's in a most wonderful old village called Alt-Lübars, and you never guess it's so near a big city. There are guaranteed only real Germans in this place, straight out of a wartime American propaganda movie! The food is so-so, but the beer is great.

The hotel in Das Exil, reports Newton is a bit funky.

Henne means chicken--the best.

Drink a "schorle" ice cold or a Berliner weisse. Typical. The first is white wine & soda, the 2nd white beer (low alcohol) with a shot of raspberry--refreshing.
Henne is right smack against the Wall. Here you'll find Berlin's absolutely guaranteed best fried chicken. You can eat the bones, too. Dates from the late 19th century, run by a young couple who used to be customers there. When the owners got too old, they bought it from them. The couple's name is Henne, which means chicken. Funny, no? There's also a very special schnapps you should try. The bill is ridiculously low. But RESERVE.
Off the Ku'damm in the Grolmanstr. is a bar that is a must. Called Diener's, it carries the name of an old Berlin boxer who was its owner. It's real heavy on the most guaranteed genuine Berliner "atmosphere." Stick to drinking and don't eat there. I took Billy Wilder to Diener's while he was in Berlin being made

Old Lucci Sylvano at the Bovril bar.

**34**

Frau Glencke, Newton's host at the special Askanischer Hof.

an honorary professor. Billy almost cried with nostalgia and stayed until 2 a.m. He who is generally in bed at home in L.A. real early.
Bovril is a civilised restaurant and bar. The food's just OK, but the barmaid is terrific, as you can see, and many years and her name is Sylvana. She's gone now, but her spirit lingers on.
Bel ami is frankly a bordello, one of quite a few in Berlin, absolutely OK with the authorities, so you risk nothing on a legal level. It has a bar and you are not obligated to have a girl. There is an indoor pool, and 2 of the private rooms are amusing--specially, I seem to remember, No. 2, with a kind of futuristic 60's bed. On my visit the girls told me that the joint is still jumping at 10 in the morning. The boss is very

The bar is great in Alt-Lübars.

It's called Bel Ami, and it's a bordello.

nice and it's a relaxed place, he's called Detlef Ullmann. Address, Reichssportfeldstr. 14.
Das Exil is well known. Very amusing people, great atmosphere--not quite like my stamp. Food is a bit heavy, Austro-Hungarian. The bar is great and the owner charming and knowledgeable on many things. Paul Linces Uter in the Kreuzberg district is the address.
Querenlierie was pointed out to me by the curator of the Berlinische Gallerie as the gallery to watch. As yet not too well known but apparently highly promising. Address: Wriezenerstr. 35, Berlin-Wedding-65. Tel. 494-6265.
Love and kisses, Helmut

Publication **Elle**
Art Director **Phyllis Schefer**
Designer **Phyllis Schefer**
Photographer **Steven Silverstein**
Publisher **Murdoch/Hachette**
Category **Cover**
Date **July 1987**

Publication **Elle**
Art Director **Phyllis Schefer**
Designer **Phyllis Schefer**
Photographer **Gilles Bensimon**
Publisher **Murdoch/Hachette**
Category **Cover**
Date **May 1987**

Publication **Elle**
Art Director **Phyllis Schefer**
Designer **Regis Pagniez**
Photographer **Gilles Bensimon**
Publisher **Murdoch/Hachette**
Category **Cover**
Date **December 1987**

Publication **Elle**
Art Director **Phyllis Schefer**
Designer **Phyllis Schefer**
Photographer **Oliviero Toscani**
Publisher **Murdoch/Hachette**
Category **Cover**
Date **September 1987**

Publication **Rolling Stone**
Art Director **Fred Woodward**
Designer **Fred Woodward**
Photographer **Herb Ritts**
Photo Editor **Laurie Kratochvil**
Publisher **Straight Arrow Publishers**
Category **Cover**
Date **September 10, 1987**

Publication **Rolling Stone**
Art Director **Fred Woodward**
Designer **Fred Woodward**
Photographer **William Coupon**
Photo Editor **Laurie Kratochvil**
Publisher **Straight Arrow Publishers**
Category **Cover**
Date **October 1987**

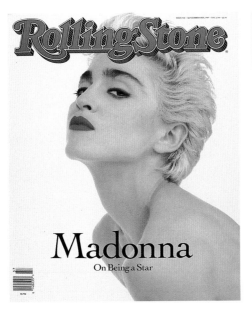 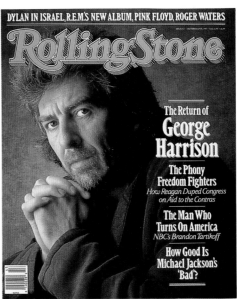

 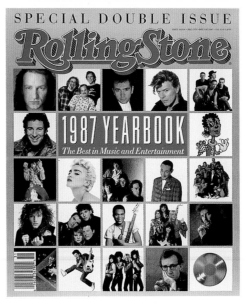

Publication **Rolling Stone**
Art Director **Fred Woodward**
Designer **Fred Woodward**
Illustrator **Anita Kunz**
Publisher **Straight Arrow Publishers**
Category **Cover**
Date **September 24, 1987**

Publication **Rolling Stone**
Art Director **Fred Woodward**
Designer **Fred Woodward**
Photo Editor **Laurie Kratochvil**
Publisher **Straight Arrow Publishers**
Category **Cover**
Date **December 17-31, 1987**

Publication **San Francisco Focus**
Art Director **Matthew Drace**
Designer **Matthew Drace**
Illustrator **Anita Kunz**
Publisher **KQED**
Category **Cover**
Date **July 1987**

Publication **San Francisco Focus**
Art Director **Matthew Drace**
Designer **Matthew Drace**
Illustrator **Seymour Chwast**
Publisher **KQED**
Category **Cover**
Date **November 1987**

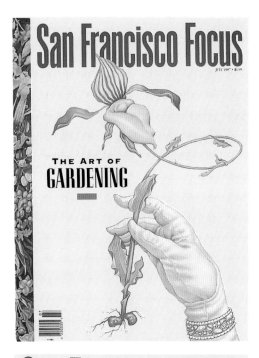

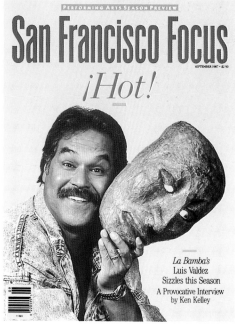

Publication **San Francisco Focus**
Art Director **Matthew Drace**
Designer **Matthew Drace**
Photographer **Stefano Massei**
Publisher **KQED**
Category **Cover**
Date **October 1987**

Publication **San Francisco Focus**
Art Director **Matthew Drace**
Designer **Matthew Drace**
Photographer **Elizabeth Zeilon**
Publisher **KQED**
Category **Cover**
Date **September 1987**

Publication **Spy**
Art Director **Alexander Isley**
Designer **Alexander Isley**
Photographer **Ron Galella**
Photo Editor **Amy Stark**
Publisher **Spy Publishing Partners**
Category **Cover**
Date **May 1987**

Publication **Spy**
Art Director **Alexander Isley**
Designer **Alexander Isley**
Photographers **Neil Selkirk, Dennis Brack**
Photo Editor **Amy Stark**
Publisher **Spy Publishing Partners**
Category **Cover**
Date **November 1987**

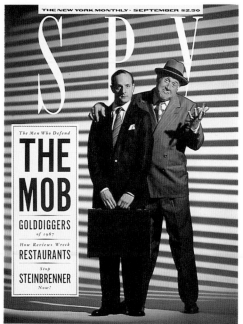

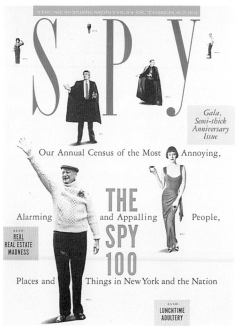

Publication **Spy**
Art Director **Alexander Isley**
Designer **Alexander Isley**
Photographer **Chris Callis**
Publisher **Spy Publishing Partners**
Category **Cover**
Date **September 1987**

Publication **Spy**
Art Director **Alexander Isley**
Designer **Alexander Isley**
Photo Editor **Amy Stark**
Publisher **Spy Publishing Partners**
Category **Cover**
Date **October 1987**

Publication **Texas Monthly**
Art Director **D.J. Stout**
Designer **D.J. Stout**
Photographer **William Coupon**
Photo Editor **D.J. Stout**
Publisher **Texas Monthly**
Category **Cover**
Date **November 1987**

Publication **Scene**
Art Director **Edward Leida**
Designers **Owen Hartley, Edward Leida, Kirby Rodriquez**
Photographer **Phillipe Costes**
Publisher **Fairchild Publications**
Category **Cover**
Date **December 1987**

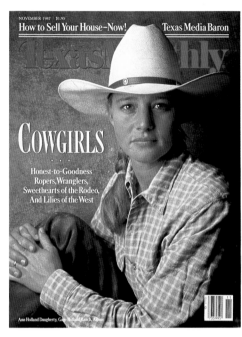

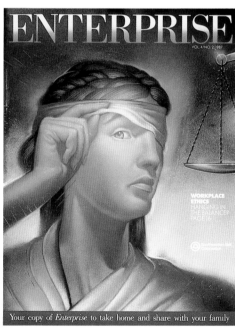

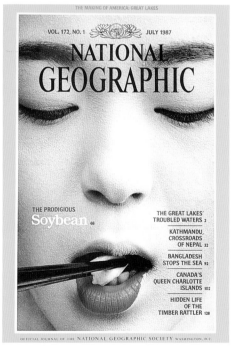

Publication **Enterprise**
Art Director **John Howze**
Designer **John Howze**
Illustrator **Cary Henrie**
Illustration Editor **Douglas Wolfe**
Client **Southwestern Bell Corporation**
Agency **Hawthorne/Wolfe Design**
Category **Cover**
Date **June 1987**

Publication **National Georgraphic**
Art Director **Gerard A. Valerio**
Designer **Wilbur E. Garrett**
Photographer **Chris Johns**
Photo Editor **Susan Welchman**
Publisher **National Geographic Society**
Category **Cover**
Date **July 1987**

Publication **New York**
Art Director **Robert Best**
Designer **Betsy Welsh**
Photographer **David Kelley**
Publisher **News Group America**
Category **Cover**
Date **November 1987**

Publication **New York**
Art Director **Robert Best**
Designer **Josh Gosfield**
Illustrator **Max Ginsburg**
Publisher **News Group America Categor Cover**
Date **December 1987**

Publication **New York**
Art Director **Robert Best**
Photographer **Jon Jensen**
Photo Editor **Jordan Schaps**
Publisher **News Group America**
Category **Cover**
Date **September 1987**

40

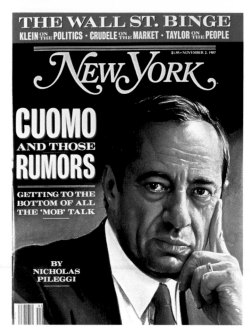

Publication **New York**
Art Director **Robert Best**
Designer **Josh Gosfield**
Photographer **Douglas Kirkland/Sygma**
Publisher **News Group America**
Category **Cover**
Date **September 21, 1987**

Publication **New York**
Art Director **Robert Best**
Illustrator **Alan Reingold**
Publisher **News Group America**
Category **Cover**
Date **November 1987**

Publication **New York**
Art Director **Robert Best**
Designer **Josh Gosfield**
Illustrator **Gary Hallgren**
Publisher **News Group America**
Category **Cover**
Date **December 1987**

Publication **Condé Nast's Traveler**
Art Director **Lloyd Ziff**
Designer **Richard Pandiscio**
Photographer **Helmut Newton**
Photo Editor **Kathleen Klech**
Publisher **Condé Nast Publications, Inc.**
Category **Cover**
Date **October 1987**

Publication **Connoisseur**
Art Director **Sandra Di Pasqua**
Designer **Sandra Di Pasqua**
Photo Editor **Phyllis Levine**
Publisher **The Hearst Corporation**
Category **Cover**
Date **August 1987**

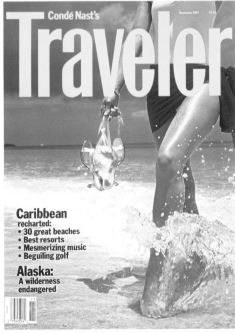

Publication **Condé Nast's Traveler**
Art Director **Lloyd Ziff**
Designer **Richard Paudiscio**
Photographer **Hiro**
Photo Editor **Kathleen Klech**
Publisher **Condé Nast Publications, Inc.**
Category **Cover**
Date **November 1987**

Publication **Connoisseur**
Art Director **Sandra Di Pasqua**
Designer **Sandra Di Pasqua**
Photo Editor **Phyllis Levine**
Publisher **The Hearst Corporation**
Category **Cover**
Date **December 1987**

Publication **Florida**
Art Director **Santa Choplin**
Designer **Santa Choplin**
Illustrator **Earl Keleny**
Publisher **The Orlando Sentinel**
Category **Cover**
Date **January 18, 1987**

Publication **Industry Update '87**
Art Director **Terry Ross Koppel**
Designer **Terry Ross Koppel**
Client **Queens Group**
Agency **Koppel & Scher**
Category **Cover**
Date **May 1987**

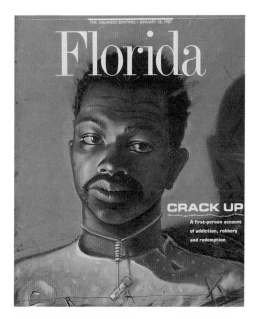

42

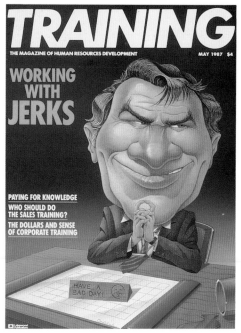

Publication **Training**
Art Director **Jodi Scharff**
Designer **Jodi Scharff**
Illustrator **Doug Oudekerk**
Publisher **Lakewood Publications**
Category **Cover**
Date **May 1987**

Publication **Graphics Arts Monthly**
Art Director **Karen Lehrer**
Designer **Karen Lehrer**
Photographer **Peter Neumann**
Publisher **Cahners Publishing**
Category **Cover**
Date **November 1987**

Publication **Fortune**
Art Director **Margery Peters**
Designer **Renee Klein**
Illustrator **Edward Sorel**
Publisher **The Hearst Corporation**
Category **Cover**
Date **July 6, 1987**

Publication **Artforum**
Art Director **Tibor Kalman**
Designer **Emily Oberman**
Photo Editor **Melissa Harris**
Client **Artforum**
Agency **M & Co.**
Category **Cover**
Date **November 1987**

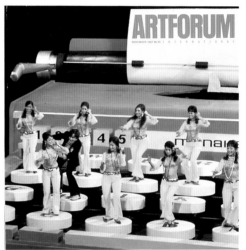

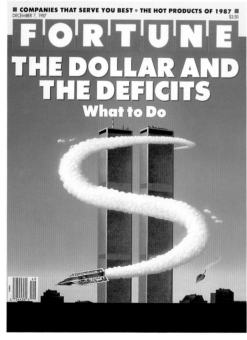

43

Publication **Fortune**
Art Director **Margery Peters**
Designer **Margery Peters**
Illustrator **Robert Crawford**
Publisher **The Hearst Corporation**
Category **Cover**
Date **December 1987**

Publication **The Lamp**
Art Director **John J. Conley**
Designers **John J. Conley, David L. Bull**
Photographer **John J. Conley**
Publisher **Exxon Corporation**
Category **Cover**
Date **Spring 1987**

Publication **Metropolis**
Art Director **Helene Silverman**
Designer **Helene Silverman**
Illustrator **Helene Silverman**
Publisher **Metropolis Magazine**
Category **Cover**
Date **October 1987**

Publication **Chicago**
Art Director **Cynthia Hoffman**
Designer **Barbara Solowan**
Photographer **Dennis Manarchy**
Publisher **Metropolitan Communications, Ltd.**
Category **Cover**
Date **September 1987**

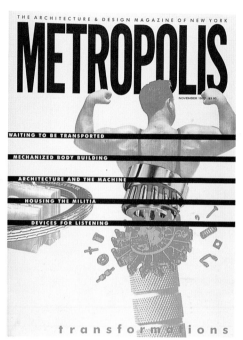

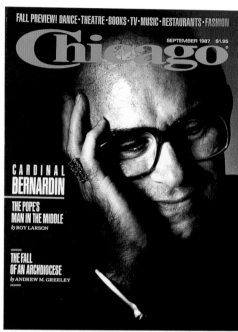

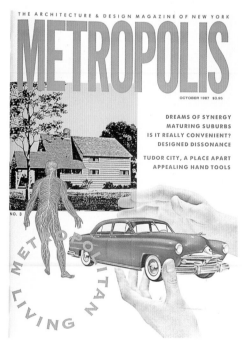

Publication **Metropolis**
Art Director **Helene Silverman**
Designer **Helene Silverman**
Illustrator **Helene Silverman**
Publisher **Metropolis Magazine**
Category **Cover**
Date **November 1987**

Publication **Connecticut's Finest**
Art Director **Deb Hardison**
Design Director **Bett McLean**
Photographer **Hans Neleman**
Publisher **Whittle Communications**
Category **Cover**
Date **Summer 1986**

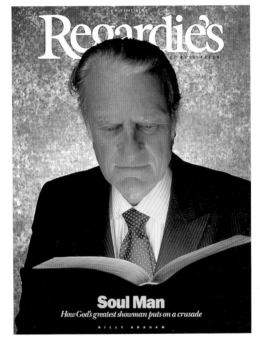

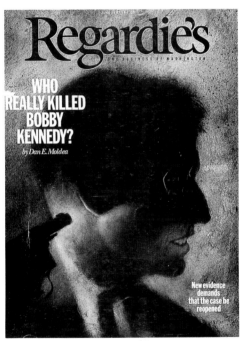

Publication **Regardie's**
Art Director **Fred Woodward**
Designers **Jolene Cuyler, Fred Woodward**
Photographer **Nigel Dickson**
Publisher **Regardie's**
Category **Cover**
Date **May 1987**

Publication **Regardie's**
Art Director **Fred Woodward**
Designers **Jolene Cuyler, Fred Woodward**
Illustrator **Matt Mahurin**
Publisher **Regardie's**
Category **Cover**
Date **June 1987**

Publication **Regardie's**
Art Director **Fred Woodward**
Designers **Jolene Cuyler, Fred Woodward**
Photographer **Nigel Dickson**
Publisher **Regardie's**
Category **Cover**
Date **July 1987**

Publication **Auto Gallery**
Art Director **Michael Brock**
Designer **Michael Brock**
Photographer **Cindy Lewis**
Publisher **Auto Gallery Publishing Co.**
Category **Cover**
Date **June 1987**

Publication **Auto Gallery**
Art Director **Michael Brock**
Designer **Michael Brock**
Photographer **Cindy Lewis**
Publisher **Auto Gallery Publishing Co.**
Category **Cover**
Date **August 1987**

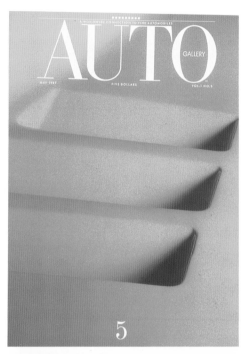

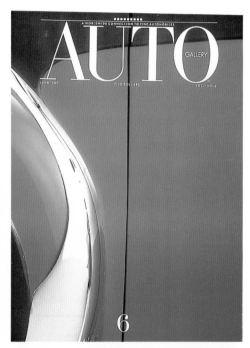

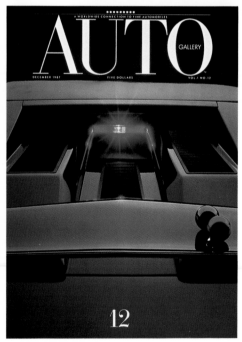

Publication **Auto Gallery**
Art Director **Michael Brock**
Designer **Michael Brock**
Photographer **Bruce Miller**
Publisher **Auto Gallery Publishing Co.**
Category **Cover**
Date **November 1987**

Publication **Auto Gallery**
Art Director **Michael Brock**
Designer **Michael Brock**
Photographer **John Paul Endress**
Publisher **Auto Gallery Publishing Co.**
Category **Cover**
Date **December 1987**

Publication **Town & Country**
Art Director **Melissa Tardiff**
Designer **Richard Turtletaub**
Illustrator **John Rombola**
Photographer **Cy Gross**
Publisher **The Hearst Corporation**
Category **Cover**
Date **January 1987**

Publication **Maryland**
Art Director **Liz Clark**
Designer **Liz Clark**
Photographer **Cappy Jackson**
Photo Editors **Liz Clark, Patrick Hornberger**
Publisher **State of Maryland**
Category **Cover**
Date **Winter 1987**

Publication **Kansas City**
Art Director **John Muller**
Designer **John Muller**
Photographer **Mike Regnier**
Publisher **Kansas City Magazine**
Category **Cover**
Date **March 1987**

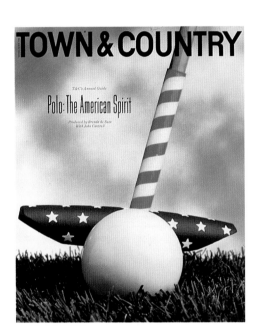
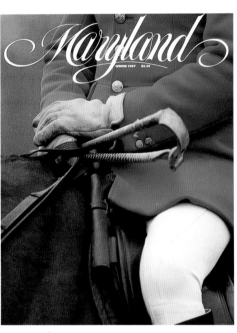
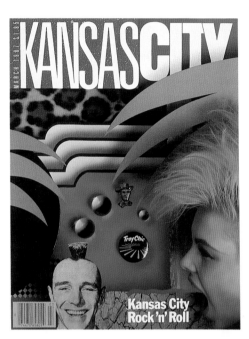

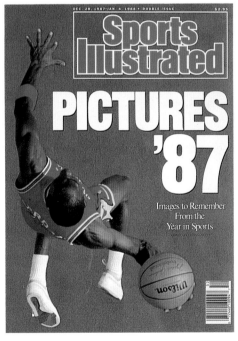
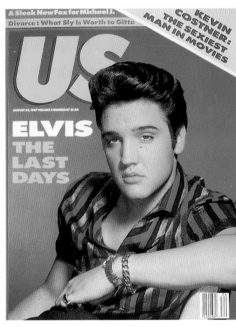

Publication **Sports Illustrated**
Art Director **Steven Hoffman**
Designer **Steven Hoffman**
Photographer **Various**
Publisher **Time, Inc.**
Category **Cover**
Date **December 1987**

Publication **Us Magazine**
Art Director **Robert Priest**
Designer **Robert Priest**
Publisher **Us Magazine Co.**
Category **Cover**
Date **August 24, 1987**

Publication **Time**
Art Directors **Rudy Hoglund, Nigel Holmes**
Designer **Nigel Holmes**
Illustrator **Michael Doret**
Photographer **Roberto Brosan**
Publisher **Time, Inc.**
Category **Cover**
Date **August 3, 1987**

Publication **Caring**
Art Directors **Mark Geer, Richard Kilmer**
Designers **Mark Geer, Richard Kilmer**
Illustrator **Regan Dunnick**
Publisher **Memorial Care Systems**
Agency **Kilmer / Geer Design**
Category **Cover**
Date **June 1987**

Publication **Business Outlook**
Art Director **Joe McNeill**
Designer **Joe McNeill**
Photographer **Danuta Otfinowski**
Publisher **CMP Publications**
Category **Cover**
Date **December 1987**

48

Publication **Caring**
Art Directors **Mark Geer, Richard Kilmer**
Designers **Mark Geer, Richard Kilmer**
Photographer **Michael Hallaway**
Client **Memorial Care Systems**
Agency **Kilmer / Geer Design**
Category **Cover**
Date **October 1987**

Publication **Plastic Surgeon**
Art Director **Steve Liska**
Designers **Sharon Zavacki, Paul Yalowitz**
Client **American Society of Plastic & Reconstructive Surgeons**
Agency **Liska & Associates**
Category **Cover**
Date **March / May 1987**

Publication **I.D.**
Art Director **Clive Jacobson**
Designer **Clive Jacobson**
Illustrator **Clive Jacobson**
Publisher **Design Publications, Inc.**
Category **Cover**
Date **March / April 1987**

Publication **Industrial Launderer**
Art Director **Jack Lefkowitz**
Designer **Jack Lefkowitz**
Illustrator **Tim Flatt**
Client **Institute of Industrial Launderers**
Agency **Jack Lefkowitz, Inc.**
Category **Cover**
Date **May 15, 1987**

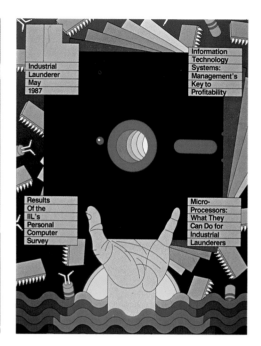

Publication **I.D.**
Art Director **Clive Jacobson**
Designer **Clive Jacobson**
Photographer **Various**
Publisher **Design Publications, Inc.**
Category **Cover**
Date **January / February 1987**

Publication **Industrial Launderer**
Art Director **Jack Lefkowitz**
Designer **Jack Lefkowitz**
Illustrator **Tim Flatt**
Photographer **David Ritchey**
Photo Editor **Jack Lefkowitz**
Client **Institute of Industrial Launderers**
Agency **Jack Lefkowitz, Inc.**
Category **Cover**
Date **July 1987**

Publication **Scholastic Math**
Art Director **Joan Michael**
Designer **Scott Frommer**
Design Director **Will Kefauver**
Publisher **Scholastic Inc.**
Category **Cover**
Date **February 13, 1987**

Publication **Scholastic Math**
Art Director **Joan Michael**
Designer **Scott Frommer**
Design Director **Will Kefauver**
Photographer **Susan Midleton**
Publisher **Scholastic Inc.**
Category **Cover**
Date **January 30, 1987**

Publication **Scholastic Math**
Art Director **Joan Michael**
Designer **Scott Frommer**
Design Director **Will Kefauver**
Photographer **Bob Lorenz**
Publisher **Scholastic Inc.**
Category **Cover**
Date **April 3, 1988**

GENERIC ISSUE
**ONE MATH MAGAZINE**
Net Wt. 26.5 g (.9275 oz.)

**PERCENTAGE OF U.S. RECOMMENDED DAILY ALLOWANCES (U.S. RDA):**

CONSUMER MATH .......100
PROBLEM SOLVING......100
FRACTIONS .............100
GEOMETRY .............100
RATIOS/PROPORTIONS ..100
VITAMIN A ...............*
VITAMIN C ...............*
CALCIUM .................*
WOOD PULP .............**
INK ......................**
GLUE ....................**

*CONTAINS LESS THAN 1% OF THE U.S. RDA OF THESE NUTRIENTS

**NOT RECOMMENDED FOR HUMAN CONSUMPTION

THIS PRODUCT IS SOLD BY VOLUME, NOT WEIGHT.

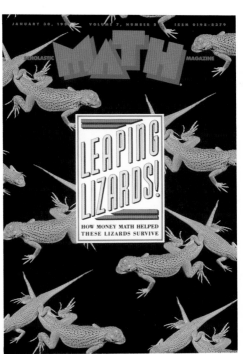

LEAPING LIZARDS!

HOW MONEY MATH HELPED THESE LIZARDS SURVIVE

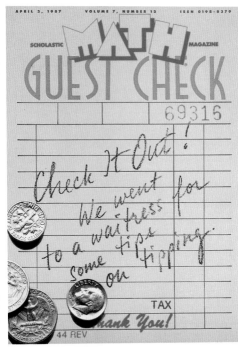

GUEST CHECK

69316

Check It Out! We went to a waitress for some tips on tipping.

TAX

Thank You!

44 REV

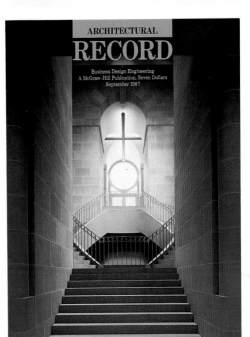

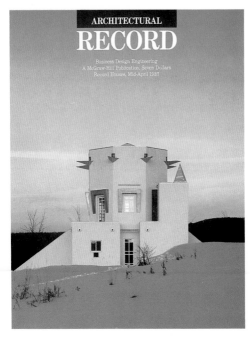

Publication **Architectural Record**
Art Director **Alberto Bucchianeri**
Designer **Alberto Bucchianeri**
Photographer **Nick Wheeler**
Publisher **McGraw-Hill, Inc.**
Category **Cover**
Date **September 1987**

Publication **Architectural Record**
Art Director **Alberto Bucchianeri**
Designer **Alberto Bucchianeri**
Photographer **Paul Warchol**
Publisher **McGraw-Hill, Inc.**
Category **Cover**
Date **January 1987**

Publication **Architectural Record**
Art Director **Alberto Bucchianeri**
Designer **Alberto Bucchianeri**
Photographer **Mick Hales**
Publisher **McGraw-Hill, Inc.**
Category **Cover**
Date **Mid-April 1987**

Publication **Varbusines**
Art Director **Joe McNeill**
Designers **Joe McNeill, Jim Wilson**
Photographer **Hashi**
Publisher **CMP Publications Inc.**
Category **Cover**

Publication **Teen-Age Magazine**
Art Director **Robin Poosikian**
Designer **Robin Poosikian**
Photographer **Beth Baptiste**
Publisher **Computer Publishing Services, Inc.**
Category **Cover**
Date **May 1987**

Publication **Scholastic News**
Art Director **Tony DeLuna**
Designer **Peggy Golden**
Design Director **Will Kefauver**
Illustrator **Justin Novak**
Publisher **Scholastic Inc.**
Category **Cover**
Date **December 4, 1987**

Publication **Teen-Age Magazine**
Art Director **Robin Poosikian**
Designer **Robin Poosikian**
Photographer **Beth Baptiste**
Publisher **Computer Publishing Services, Inc.**
Category **Cover**
Date **July 1987**

Publication **Pacific**
Art Director **Michael Mabry**
Designers **Michael Mabry, Renee Holsen**
Illustrator **Guy Billout**
Illustration Editor **Teresa Ruano**
Client **Pacific Telesis**
Agency **Michael Mabry Design, Inc.**
Category **Cover**
Date **January 1987**

Publication **House & Garden**
Art Director **Karen Lee Grant**
Designer **Karen Lee Grant**
Photographer **Jacques Dirand**
Photo Editor **Tom McWilliam**
Publisher **Conde Nast Publications, Inc.**
Category **Cover**
Date **December 1987**

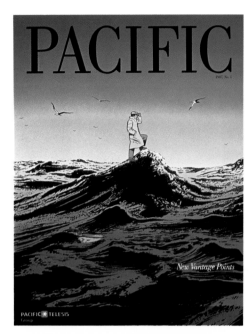

**52**

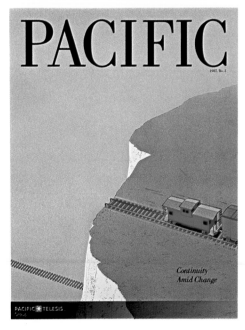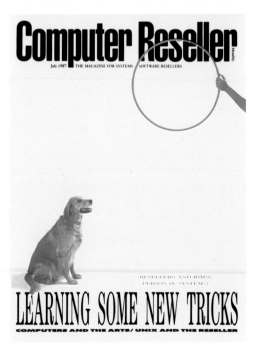

Publication **Pacific**
Art Director **Michael Mabry**
Designers **Michael Mabry, Piper Murakami**
Illustrator **Guy Billout**
Illustration Editor **Teresa Ruano**
Client **Pacific Telesis**
Agency **Michael Mabry Design, Inc.**
Category **Cover**
Date **August 1987**

Publication **Computer Reseller**
Art Director **Michael Walters**
Designer **Michael Walters**
Photographer **Glenn Killian**
Publisher **International Thomson Retail Press**
Category **Cover**
Date **July 1987**

Publication **The Washington Post Magazine**
Art Director **Brian Noyes**
Designer **Brian Noyes**
Illustrator **Stan Watts**
Photo Editor **Molly Roberts**
Publisher **The Washington Post**
Category **Cover**
Date **July 1987**

Publication **Directions**
Art Director **Howard Greenwald**
Designer **Wynne Medinger**
Photographer **George Kamper**
Publisher **IBM Corporation**
Category **Cover**
Date **Summer 1987**

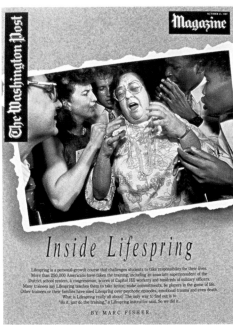

Publication **The Washington Post Magazine**
Art Director **Brian Noyes**
Designer **Brian Noyes**
Photographer **Mary Ellen Mark**
Photo Editor **Molly Roberts**
Publisher **The Washington Post**
Category **Cover**
Date **October 1987**

Publication **New Lincoln School**
Art Director **Fausto Pellegrini**
Designer **Nadia Pignatone**
Client **New Lincoln School**
Agency **Jan Krukowski Associates**
Category **Cover**
Date **September 1987**

Publication **The Boston Globe Magazine**
Art Director **Lacy Bartholomay**
Designer **Lucy Bartholomay**
Illustrator **Patrick Blackwell**
Publisher **The Boston Globe**
Category **Cover**
Date **November 23, 1987**

Publication **The Boston Globe Magazine**
Art Director **Lucy Bartholomay**
Designer **Lucy Bartholomay**
Photographer **Keith Jenkins**
Publisher **Boston Globe**
Category **Cover**
Date **December 13, 1987**

Publication **The Boston Globe Magazine**
Art Director **Lucy Bartholomay**
Designer **Lucy Bartholomay**
Publisher **The Boston Globe**
Category **Cover**
Date **August 23, 1987**

### The Problem

It started in the garden.
Eve said to Adam:
"We need to talk."
Adam said to Eve:
"What's to talk? We did that
the day we got the fig leaves."
And there's been trouble ever since.

BY SUSAN TRAUSCH

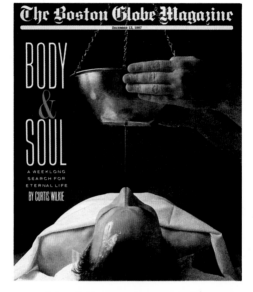

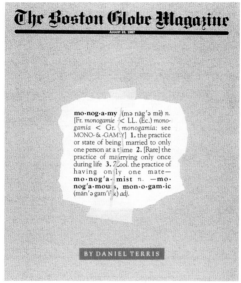

54

Publication **The East-West Papers**
Art Director **Jurek Wajdowicz**
Designer **Jurek Wajdowicz**
Photographer **Mark Sands**
Client **The East-West Round Table**
Agency **Emerson, Wajdowicz Studios, Inc.**
Category **Cover**
Date **February 1, 1987**

Publication **The East-West Papers**
Art Director **Jurek Wajdowicz**
Designer **Jurek Wajdowicz**
Photographer **Robert Gale**
Client **The East-West Round Table**
Agency **Emerson, Wajdowski Studios, Inc.**
Category **Cover**
Date **September / October 1987**

Publication **Chicago Tribune / Tempo Woman**
Art Director **Mare Earley**
Designer **Mare Earley**
Illustrator **David Suter**
Publisher **Chicago Tribune**
Category **Cover**
Date **January 11, 1987**

Publication **The New York Times / Travel Section**
Art Director **Greg Ryan**
Designer **Greg Ryan**
Illustrator **Nancy Doniger**
Publisher **The New York Times**
Category **Cover**
Date **April 12, 1987**

Publication **The New York Times / Arts & Leisure**
Art Director **Linda Brewer**
Designer **Linda Brewer**
Photographer **Various**
Publisher **The New York Times**
Category **Cover**
Date **December 27, 1987**

Publication **The New York Times / Home Section**
Art Director **Nicki Kalish**
Designer **Nicki Kalish**
Illustrator **Jim Ludtke**
Publisher **The New York Times**
Category **Cover**
Date **May 7, 1987**

Publication **The New York Times / Sports Section**
Art Director **Michael Valenti**
Designer **Michael Valenti**
Illustrator **Michael Klein**
Photographer **Associated Press**
Publisher **The New York Times**
Category **Cover**
Date **February 2, 1987**

Publication **New York**
Art Director **Robert Best**
Designers **Josh Gosfield, Betsy Welsh**
Photographer **Michael Skott**
Photo Editor **Jordan Schaps**
Publisher **News Group America**
Category **Single Page / Spread**
Date **May 18, 1987**

Publication **New York**
Art Director **Robert Best**
Designers **Josh Gosfield, Betsy Welsh**
Photographer **Jon Jensen**
Photo Editor **Jordan Schaps**
Publisher **News Group America**
Category **Single Page / Spread**
Date **September 28, 1987**

Publication **New York**
Art Director **Robert Best**
Designers **Josh Gosfield, Betsy Welsh**
Illustrator **William Hamilton**
Publisher **News Group America**
Category **Single Page / Spread**
Date **November 23, 1987**

Publication **New York**
Art Director **Robert Best**
Designer **Josh Gosfield**
Illustrator **Brian Cronin**
Publisher **News Group America**
Category **Single Page / Spread**
Date **December 1987**

# HATS ON
BY WENDY GOODMAN

# JUST FOR THE FUN OF IT
BY WENDY GOODMAN

# ALL THE TRIMMINGS

PHOTOGRAPHED BY SANTE D'ORAZIO

Publication **New York**
Art Director **Robert Best**
Designers **Robert Best, Deborah Quintana**
Photographer **Just Loomis**
Publisher **News Group America**
Category **Single Page / Spread**
Date **February 16, 1987**

Publication **New York**
Art Director **Robert Best**
Designers **Josh Gosfield, Betsy Welsh**
Photographer **Andrea Blanch**
Publisher **News Group America**
Category **Single Page / Spread**
Date **August 24, 1987**

Publication **New York**
Art Director **Robert Best**
Designer **Josh Gosfield**
Photographer **Sante D'Orazio**
Publisher **News Group America**
Category **Single Page / Spread**
Date **August 24, 1987**

Publication **San Francisco Focus**
Art Director **Matthew Drace**
Designer **Matthew Drace**
Photographer **David Peterson**
Publisher **KQED**
Category **Single Page / Spread**
Date **September 1, 1987**

Publication **San Francisco Focus**
Art Director **Matthew Drace**
Designer **Matthew Drace**
Photographer **David Peterson**
Publisher **KQED**
Category **Single Page / Spread**
Date **September 1, 1987**

Publication **San Francisco Focus**
Art Director **Matthew Drace**
Designer **Matthew Drace**
Photographer **David Peterson**
Publisher **KQED**
Category **Story Presentation**
Date **September 1, 1987**

58

SYLVESTER

JOANNA BERMAN

RINDE ECKERT

# READERS, ENVELOPE *Please*

BY JACQUELINE KILLEEN AND SHARON SILVA

All year long we reviewers have had the floor in the great Bay Area restaurant debate. Now we've heard your ⌖ side. Tallying the ballots tells us as much about you, our readers, as it does about your favorite restaurants. ⌖ You're strong on eateries born in the past decade; only a handful of the winners are into their teens. And you seem to be steadfastly loyal to the same places, year after year. Yet there are some ✦ surprise winners in the poll – including a few restaurants that ✦ have been around barely a year. We learned that you speak your mind, too. Our omission of categories for American and Cambodian cuisines brought justifiably outraged grumbles from the fans of Cajun cooking, the Cambodia House restaurant and Campton Place. Our apologies; we hereby award write-in first places to both.

SAN FRANCISCO FOCUS                    FINE DINING GUIDE 11

*wristwatching*

DOES ANYBODY KNOW WHAT TIME IT IS? DOES ANYBODY REALLY CARE? WELL, SURE, BUT THESE DAYS WATCHES ARE REVEALING A LOT MORE THAN THE HOUR. KEEP YOUR EYES ON PEOPLE'S WRISTS. PLASTICS, ANTIQUES, HIGH-TECH TIMERS — THEY'RE ALL PART OF THE WATCH WARDROBE. OF COURSE, YOU CAN ALSO WEAR SEVERAL WATCHES AT THE SAME TIME.

*eyesighting*

GONE ARE THE DAYS WHEN ONE PAIR OF GLASSES GOT YOU THROUGH THE YEAR. NOW IT'S A DIFFERENT FRAME EVERY FEW HOURS — ONE LOOK FOR WORK, ANOTHER FOR SPORTS AND SOMETHING REALLY ELEGANT FOR SPECIAL NIGHTS ON THE TOWN. EYEGLASSES HAVE BECOME "JEWELRY FOR THE FACE," SO EVEN THOSE WITH 20/20 VISION ARE GETTING FRAMED.

---

Publication **San Francisco Focus**
Art Director **Matthew Drace**
Designer **Mark Ulriksen**
Illustrator **Tim Carroll**
Publisher **KQED**
Category **Story Presentation**
Date **August 1, 1987**

Publication **San Francisco Focus**
Art Director **Matthew Drace**
Designer **Mark Ulriksen**
Photographer **Thomas Heinser**
Publisher **KQED**
Category **Single Page / Spread**
Date **October 1, 1987**

Publication **San Francisco Focus**
Art Director **Matthew Drace**
Designer **Mark Ulriksen**
Photographer **Thomas Heinser**
Publisher **KQED**
Category **Single Page / Spread**
Date **October 1, 1987**

Publication **San Francisco Focus**
Art Director **Matthew Drace**
Designer **Mark Ulriksen**
Publisher **Anthony Russo**
Publisher **KQED**
Category **Single Page / Spread**
Date **October 1, 1987**

Publication **San Francisco Focus**
Art Director **Matthew Drace**
Designer **Mark Ulriksen**
Photographer **George Lange**
Publisher **KQED**
Category **Single Page / Spread**
Date **December 1, 1987**

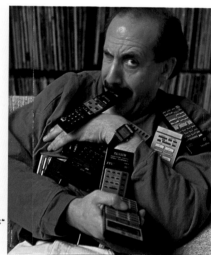

Publication **San Francisco Focus**
Art Director **Matthew Drace**
Designer **Mark Ulriksen**
Illustrator **Matt Mahurin**
Publisher **KQED**
Category **Single Page / Spread**
Date **December 1, 1987**

Publication **San Francisco Focus**
Art Director **Matthew Drace**
Designer **Mark Ulriksen**
Illustrator **Philippe Weisbecker**
Publisher **KQED**
Category **Single Page / Spread**
Date **November 1, 1987**

Publication **Regardie's**

Art Directors **Fred Woodward, Jolene Cuyler**

Designer **Jolene Cuyler**

Illustrator **Peter De Seve**

Publisher **Regardie's**

Category **Story Presentation**

Date **May 1987**

Publication **Regardie's**

Art Directors **Fred Woodward, Jolene Cuyler**

Designer **Jolene Cuyler**

Illustrator **Mark Marek**

Publisher **Regardie's**

Category **Story Presentation**

Date **July 1987**

Publication **Spy**
Art Director **Alexander Isley**
Designer **Alexander Isley**
Photo Editor **Amy Stark**
Publisher **Spy Publishing Partners**
Category **Single Page / Spread**
Date **June 1987**

Publication **Spy**
Art Director **Alexander Isley**
Designer **Alexander Isley**
Photographer **Marina Garnier**
Photo Editor **Amy Stark**
Publisher **Spy Publishing Partners**
Category **Single Page / Spread**
Date **September 1987**

GOOD novelists, BAD novelists — they're all chumps unless they're best-selling novelists. As far as we're concerned, nothing but high-priced fiction will do, whether it's an Elmore Leonard ($1.5 million per mystery), a John Jakes ($4 million per bad historical epic) or a James Clavell ($5 million per really bad historical epic). So come along now, as soon-to-be-best-selling author ELLIS WEINER (Decade of the Year, E. P. Dutton) takes us on an all-star, all-expenses-paid tour of the

# PROSE STYLES of the RICH and FAMOUS

IN A HUNDRED DIFFERENT TONGUES of a thousand different places; on the grandest themes or the smallest of subjects; intended for all of humanity throughout history or for an esoteric enclave existing ephemerally for an evanescent instant — these are the prose styles of the rich and famous. Come with us on a whirlwind tour, as we taste of the achievements in leitmotiv and language, content and concept, imagery and imagination, that have increased by an incalculable increment the collective culture and literary legacy of all mankind.

For many people, life is a series of high-stakes business deals, ferociously pursued including courtship and marriage. Yes, this is 1987; loveless marriage is chic again. And even though we, like you, find the whole business appalling and sad and sordid and vulgar, once we started, we couldn't stop listening to HELL SCOVELL explain

*How to Marry a*

Gayfryd Steinberg grew up in a rented house in Vancouver, British Columbia, the daughter of a telephone company clerk. Today she lives with her husband, the overfed conglomerateur Saul Steinberg, in an art-clogged Park Avenue triplex that used to belong to John D. Rockefeller Jr. The apartment measures roughly 28,000 square feet, larger than Tiffany's three sales floors combined. Paintings by Titian, Rubens and Frans Hals hang in the public rooms. A lesser artist such as Renoir is placed in Gayfryd Steinberg's powder room.

Barbara "Basia" Piasecka Johnson emigrated from Poland in 1968 with

# illionaire

$100 and sufficient cleaning skills to get a chambermaid's job in the home of J. Seward Johnson, the late nutty Johnson & Johnson heir and marine biology buff. Three years later she had stopped doing windows, married her boss and begun overseeing construction of Jasna Polana ("Bright Meadow"), a $30 million Palladian mansion of wretched excess on 140 acres in Princeton, New Jersey. The grounds include a 72-foot-long swimming pool surrounded by Greek and Roman antiquities

✂ GOLD-diggers of 1987

By day they're ordinary — really ordinary — civilians. But as soon as they slip out of their workaday duds and into their authoritarian

blues, they begin their posturing and overreacting. They're make-believe

crime fighters, they're faux police, they're the goofy tagalong

kid brothers and sisters of New York's Finest, they're . . .

# THE HOBBY COPS

BY JAMES TRAUB
PHOTOGRAPHED BY ED EDAHL

19:42 HOURS (or thereabouts), June 17. Officer Robin Riccio, in civilian garb, is brushing away the crumbs as Officer Nick Diomede, a genuine police officer, polishes off the last of his sandwich. A hubbub of greetings and well-worn gibes begins to rise as men file into the tiny room in the Central Park Precinct house. Captain Stephan Peskin arrives in his business suit, ducks into a little room and reemerges in the blue uniform with the crisp white shirt that signify his rank. Diomede tilts back in his creaky swivel chair and facetiously complains about crabs in his Mr. Coffee machine. Riccio beats through a battered file cabinet. And another officer shouts, "Fall in!" The men (and woman) stop talking and line up—all four of them—and listen to the evening's patrol assignments. For the next several hours these blue-clad volunteers will harm no one while enjoying a pleasant stroll up and down the well-lit main arteries of Central Park. Perhaps they'll give directions it comes with the territory. Not much else does. The men exit into the warm summer's evening. And so begins another everyday episode of . . . Hobby Cops.

PERHAPS, WITHOUT REALIZING IT, YOU'VE seen some of these men and women marching vigilantly up and down your neighborhood avenues, preventing crimes of opportunity. They are the Auxiliary Police. They wear blue uniforms with shiny badges and shoulder patches, just like the real police, although if you look very closely you can see the word AUXILIARY on the badge and patch. Around their midsection they carry the usual clanking selection of police gear - nightstick, handcuffs, notepad, flashlight, everything except the service revolver, thank God. Some also carry bullet pouches, which look quite smart.

Who are the Auxiliaries? They're men and women just like you—lawyers and dentists, mailmen and schoolteachers. The difference

Publication **Spy**
Art Director **Alexander Isley**
Designer **Alexander Isley**
Photographer **Ed Edahl**
Photo Editor **Amy Stark**
Publisher **Spy Publishing Partners**
Category **Single Page / Spread**
Date **November 1987**

SPY has always been troubled by the very real discrimination faced by women with enormous breasts—the leering glances, the stereotyping by short-obsessed males, harassment in the workplace. Thus, the remarkable undercover investigation that follows—an article conceived, written and edited by women. It is presented not to titillate our readers, or because we thought that mentioning it on the cover would sell more copies of the magazine. No. We did it because as journalists, we have a sacred mandate to expose social injustice no matter how sensational. And so, in the ground-breaking tradition of Black Like Me and Gentleman's Agreement, LYNN SNOWDEN strapped on a pair of 34Ds for two weeks so she could personally experience the shame, the burden—and, yes, the undeniable retro glamour of being

# BUSTY LIKE me

ONE WOMAN'S TRUE STORY

FOR YEARS, the idea had intrigued me, and the day I saw Phil Donahue interview a panel of women about their breasts, it returned more insistently than ever. If a small-busted woman were to become a large-busted woman, I wondered, what adjustments would she have to make? What would it be like to receive lustful stares from men and envy or hatred from women, all as a function of breast size—something over which one has no control?

If a small-busted woman were to become a large-busted woman, would she suddenly understand, with a ferocious clarity born of painful personal experience, the daily prejudice and indignities endured by large-breasted women living in a neurotically breast-obsessed, male-dominated society? If a small-busted woman were to become a large-busted woman, would the atavistic allure of unusually large breasts cease to mystify and terrify her—or enthrall her all the more? If a small-busted woman (me, for instance) were to become a large-busted woman, would she gain invaluable insight into the psychic tics and cultural traditions that make sexuality so problematic in our society?

In other words, wouldn't it be fun to be really built?

We are in the midst, everyone must have heard by now, of a Big Breast Renaissance. Busty ▶▶

WRITER LYNN SNOWDEN

Fig 1

*"The only way to bridge the gap was to become temporarily bosomy — really bosomy. For two weeks I did everything I normally did, wore everything I normally wore. The only difference was in the Size of My Breasts"*

Publication **Spy**
Art Director **Alexander Isley**
Designer **Alexander Isley**
Photographer **Frank Schramm**
Photo Editor **Amy Stark**
Publisher **Spy Publishing Partners**
Category **Single Page / Spread**
Date **August 1987**

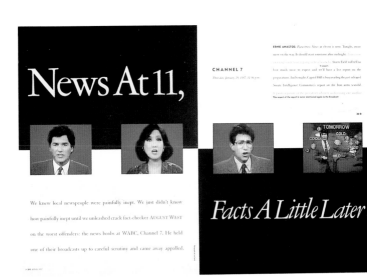

63

Publication **Spy**

Art Director **Alexander Isley**

Designer **Alexander Isley**

Photographer **Alexander Isley**

Photo Editor **Amy Stark**

Publisher **Spy Publishing Partners**

Category **Single Page/Spread**

Date **April 1987**

Publication **Spy**

Art Director **Alexander Isley**

Designer **Alexander Isley**

Photo Editor **Amy Stark**

Publisher **Spy Publishing Partners**

Category **Single Page/Spread**

Date **May 1987**

Publication **Spy**

Art Director **Alexander Isley**

Designer **Alexander Isley**

Photographer **Marina Garnier**

Photo Editor **Amy Stark**

Publisher **Spy Publishing Partners**

Category **Single Page/Spread**

Date **March 1987**

Publication **Premiere**
Art Directors **David Walters, Robert Best**
Designer **Robert Best**
Illustrators **Fred Swanson, Bill Kobasz**
Publisher **Murdoch / Hachette**
Category **Single Page / Spread**
Date **November 1987**

Publication **Premiere**
Art Directors **David Walters, Robert Best**
Designer **Robert Best**
Illustrator **Stuart Wurtzel**
Photographer **Barry Wetcher**
Publisher **Murdoch / Hachette**
Category **Single Page / Spread**
Date **November 1987**

Publication **Premiere**
Art Directors **David Walters, Robert Best**
Designers **Robert Best, David Walters**
Illustrator **Daniel Kirk**
Publisher **Murdoch / Hachette**
Category **Single Page / Spread**
Date **October 1987**

Publication **Premiere**
Art Directors **David Walters, Robert Best**
Designer **Robert Best**
Photographer **Andy Schwartz**
Publisher **Murdoch / Hachette**
Category **Single Page / Spread**
Date **December 1987**

Publication **Premiere**
Art Directors **David Walters, Robert Best**
Designers **Robert Best, David Walters**
Photographer **David Kelley**
Publisher **Murdoch / Hachette**
Category **Single Page / Spread**
Date **December 1987**

Publication **Premiere**
Art Directors **David Walters, Robert Best**
Designers **Robert Best, David Walters**
Illustrator **Gary Halgren**
Photographer **Attila Dory**
Publisher **Murdoch / Hachette**
Category **Single Page / Spread**
Date **October 1987**

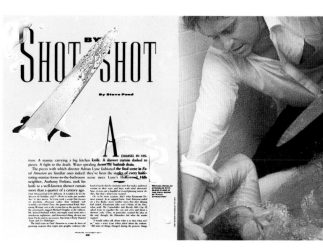

Publication **Premiere**
Art Directors **David Walters, Robert Best**
Designer **Robert Best**
Photographer **Zade Rosenthal**
Publisher **Murdoch / Hachette**
Category **Single Page / Spread**
Date **July / August 1987**

Publication **Premiere**
Art Directors **David Walters, Robert Best**
Designers **David Walters, Robert Best**
Illustrator **Fred Swanson**
Photographers **Andy Schwartz, David Kelley**
Publisher **Murdoch / Hachette**
Category **Single Page / Spread**
Date **November 1987**

Publication **Spy**
Art Director **Alexander Isley**
Designer **Alexander Isley**
Illustrator **Ross MacDonald**
Publisher **Spy Publishing Partners**
Category **Single Page / Spread**
Date **October 1987**

Publication **Premiere**
Art Directors **David Walters, Robert Best**
Designers **Robert Best, David Walters**
Illustrator **Gary Halgren**
Photographer **David Kelley**
Publisher **Murdoch / Hachette**
Category **Single Page / Spread**
Date **December 1987**

Publication **Spy**
Art Director **Alexander Isley**
Designer **Alexander Isley**
Photographer **Rob Wagner, AP / Wide World**
Photo Editor **Amy Stark**
Publisher **Spy Publishing Partners**
Category **Single Page / Spread**
Date **March 1987**

66

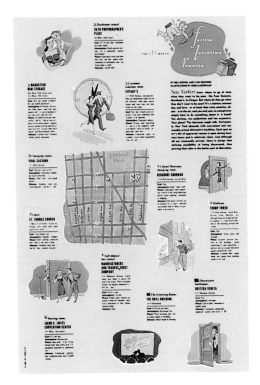

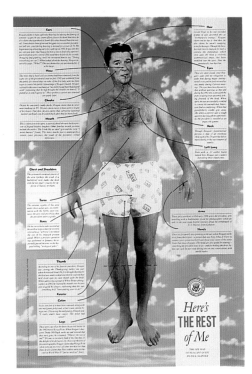

Publication **Rolling Stone**
Art Director **Fred Woodward**
Designers **Jolene Cuyler, Raul Martinez**
Photographer **Steven Meisel**
Photo Editor **Laurie Kratochvil**
Publisher **Straight Arrow Publishers**
Category **Single Page / Spread**
Date **November 5 - December 10, 1987**

Publication **Rolling Stone**
Art Director **Fred Woodward**
Designer **Karen Simpson**
Photographer **Brian Smale**
Photo Editor **Laurie Kratochvil**
Publisher **Straight Arrow Publishers**
Category **Single Page / Spread**

IN THE ISSUE

BACK IN BLACK

R.E.M

MR. CLEAN

Boy George
Straightens
Up His Act

BY MICHAEL GOLDBERG

PANAMA BANAL

THE REVOLUTION TURNS INTO AN ALL-TOO -

CIVIL WAR · BY P.J. O'ROURKE

Publication **Rolling Stone**
Art Director **Fred Woodward**
Designer **Raul Martinez**
Photographer **Deborah Feingold**
Photo Editor **Laurie Kratochvil**
Publisher **Straight Arrow Publishers**
Category **Single Page / Spread**
Date **September 24, 1987**

Publication **Rolling Stone**
Art Director **Fred Woodward**
Designer **Jolene Cuyler**
Photographer **David Bailey**
Photo Editor **Laurie Kratochvil**
Publisher **Straight Arrow Publishers**
Category **Single Page / Spread**
Date **October 8, 1987**

Publication **Rolling Stone**
Art Director **Fred Woodward**
Designer **Jolene Cuyler**
Illustrator **Jerzy Kolacz**
Publisher **Straight Arrow Publishers**
Category **Single Page / Spread**
Date **October 8, 1987**

Publication **Skateboard**
Art Director **David Carson**
Designer **David Carson**
Photographer **Grant Brittain**
Photo Editor **Grant Brittain**
Category **Single Page / Spread**
Date **December 1987**

Publication **Skateboard**
Art Director **David Carson**
Designer **David Carson**
Photographer **Grant Brittain**
Photo Editor **Grant Brittain**
Category **Single Page / Spread**
Date **August 1987**

Publication **Skateboard**
Art Director **David Carson**
Designer **David Carson**
Photographer **Yasuji Sasaki**
Photo Editor **Yasuji Sasaki**
Category **Single Page / Spread**
Date **June 1987**

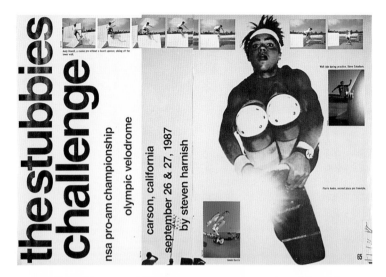

Publication **Industry Update '87**
Art Director **Terry Ross Koppel**
Designer **Terry Ross Koppel**
Client **Queens Group**
Agency **Koppel & Scher**
Category **Single Page / Spread**
Date **May 1987**

Publication **Industry Update '87**
Art Director **Terry Ross Koppel**
Designer **Terry Ross Koppel**
Client **Queens Group**
Agency **Koppel & Scher**
Category **Single Page / Spread**
Date **May 1987**

Publication **Industry Update '87**
Art Director **Terry Ross Koppel**
Designer **Terry Ross Koppel**
Client **Queens Group**
Agency **Koppel & Scher**
Category **Single Page / Spread**
Date **May 1987**

Publication **V Magazine**
Art Director **Terry Ross Koppel**
Designer **Terry Ross Koppel**
Photographer Colorization **Ralph Wernli**
Publisher **Fairfield Publications**
Category **Single Page / Spread**
Date **November 1987**

Publication **V Magazine**
Art Director **Terry Ross Koppel**
Designer **Terry Ross Koppel**
Illustrator **Rico Lins**
Publisher **Fairfield Publications**
Category **Single Page / Spread**
Date **December 1987**

Publication **V Magazine**
Art Director **Terry Ross Koppel**
Designer **Terry Ross Koppel**
Illustrator **Seymour Chwast**
Publisher **Fairfield Publications**
Category **Single Page / Spread**
Date **November 1987**

# TAKE IT Off

*Shedding pounds with the best diet videos*

By Libby Masier

**f**-bruary marks the beginning of the post-holiday payback season, when accounts must be settled with the bathroom scale. For frustrated chronic dieters, the proper video can help reinforce motivation and restore perspective, says Emily Massara, Ph.D., a Philadelphia-based medical anthropologist specializing in weight control. To help dieters choose the

*Libby Masier writes frequently on health and fitness-related topics.*

ILLUSTRATION BY DAVE CALVER

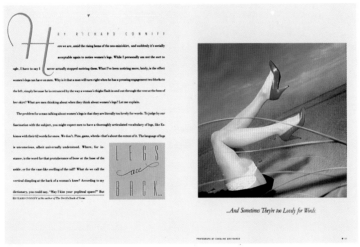

BY RICHARD CONNIFF

**H**ere we are, amid the rising hems of the neo-mini-skirt, and suddenly it's socially acceptable again to notice women's legs. While I personally am not the sort to ogle, I have to say I never actually stopped noticing them. What I've been noticing more, lately, is the effect women's legs can have on men. Why is it that a man will turn right when he has a pressing engagement two blocks to the left, simply because he is entranced by the way a woman's thighs flash in and out through the vent at the hem of her skirt? What are men thinking about when they think about women's legs? Let me explain.

The problem for a man talking about women's legs is that they are literally too lovely for words. To judge by our fascination with the subject, you might expect men to have a thoroughly articulated vocabulary of legs, like Eskimos with their 62 words for snow. We don't. Pins, gams, wheels—that's about the extent of it. The language of legs is unconscious, albeit universally understood. Where, for instance, is the word for that protuberance of bone at the base of the ankle, or for the vase-like swelling of the calf? What do we call the vertical dimpling at the back of a woman's knee? According to my dictionary, you could say, "May I kiss your popliteal space?" But

RICHARD CONNIFF is the author of The Devil's Book of Verse.

**LEGS are BACK...**

*...And Sometimes They're too Lovely for Words.*

PHOTOGRAPH BY CAROLINE GREYSHOCK

Kim, a pretty honors student, and Rick, her track-star boyfriend, are hanging out with their friends. As they chat, Kim bums a cigarette or cocaine in a minute. She offers it to Rick, who refuses it. "I'm always saying you don't want any, and then you end up having some anyway," she groans. "Why do we have to go through all this?" Embarrassed, he shrugs his shoulders and picks up his videos. *A SCENE FROM THE VIDEO SHATTERED: IF YOUR KID IS ON DRUGS.*

## A New Weapon for Parents

## FIGHTING Drugs WITH Video

By Nissa Simon

**T**hese two teenagers aren't dropouts or misfits; they are our children. The peer pressure they face, combined with the widespread availability of drugs, means they must fight the odds to stay clean. Some win; some don't. According to the National Institute on Drug Abuse, by their senior year 17 percent of all high school students have tried cocaine. Over 50 percent have tried marijuana; even more—56 percent—are active drinkers. There is a drug epidemic facing America's youth, and the overwhelming concern of many parents is how to keep their children from falling prey to it. Unfortunately, there is no simple solution. But there are ways to help kids avoid becoming involved with drugs in the first place. One of those ways is home video.

NISSA SIMON, a freelance writer specializing in health, is the author of Don't Worry, You're Normal: A Teenager's Guide to Self Health (Harper & Row).

**It's not** enough for parents to simply watch anti-drug videos with their children... they need to discuss them as well.

Publication **V Magazine**
Art Director **Terry Ross Koppel**
Designer **Terry Ross Koppel**
Illustrator **Dave Calver**
Publisher **Fairfield Publications**
Category **Single Page / Spread**
Date **December 1987**

Publication **V Magazine**
Art Director **Terry Ross Koppel**
Designer **Terry Ross Koppel**
Photographer **Caroline Greyshock**
Publisher **Fairfield Publications**
Category **Single Page / Spread**
Date **December 1987**

Publication **V Magazine**
Art Director **Terry Ross Koppel**
Designer **Terry Ross Koppel**
Illustrator **Alexa Grace**
Publisher **Fairfield Publications**
Category **Single Page / Spread**
Date **September 1987**

Publication **Eastern Review**
Art Director **Nancy Campbell**
Designer **Nancy Campbell**
Illustrator **Regan Dunnick**
Publisher **East / West Network**
Category **Single Page / Spread**
Date **March 1987**

Publication **Eastern Review**
Art Director **Nancy Campbell**
Designer **Nancy Campbell**
Photographer **Robert Llewellyn**
Publisher **East / West Network**
Category **Single Page / Spread**
Date **July 1987**

Publication **Eastern Review**
Art Director **Nancy Campbell**
Designer **Nancy Campbell**
Photographer **Charles Purvis**
Publisher **East / West Network**
Category **Single Page / Spread**
Date **July 1987**

Publication **Eastern Review**
Art Director **Nancy Campbell**
Designer **Nancy Campbell**
Illustrator **Alan E. Cober**
Publisher **East / West Network**
Category **Single Page / Spread**
Date **May 1987**

Publication **Eastern Review**
Art Director **Nancy Campbell**
Designer **Melissa Lanitis**
Illustrator **Elwood H. Smith**
Publisher **East / West Network**
Category **Single Page / Spread**
Date **May 1987**

Publication **US**
Art Director **Robert Priest**
Designer **Scott Yardley**
Photographer **Herb Ritts**
Photo Editor **Karen Silverstein**
Publisher **US Magazine**
Category **Single Page / Spread**
Date **August 10, 1987**

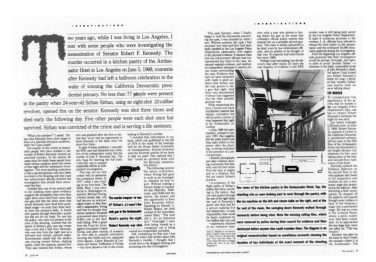

Publication **Regardie's**
Art Director **Fred Woodward**
Designer **Fred Woodward**
Publisher **Regardie's**
Category **Single Page / Spread**
Date **June 1987**

Publication **US**
Art Director **Robert Priest**
Designer **Robert Priest**
Photographers **Helmut Newton, Mark Hanauer**
Photo Editor **Karen Silverstein**
Publisher **US Magazine**
Category **Single Page / Spread**
Date **June 29, 1987**

Publication **American Health**
Art Directors **Will Hopkins, Ira Friedlander**
Designers **Will Hopkins, Ira Friedlander**
Photographer **Kathryn Kleinman**
Photo Editor **Linda Eger**
Publisher **American Health Partners**
Agency **Will Hopkins Group**
Category **Single Page / Spread**
Date **July 1987**

Publication **Conde Nast's Traveler**
Art Director **Lloyd Ziff**
Designer **Lloyd Ziff**
Illustrator **Jonathon Heale**
Photographer **James Hamilton**
Publisher **Conde Nast Publications, Inc.**
Category **Single Page / Spread**
Publisher **September 1987**

74

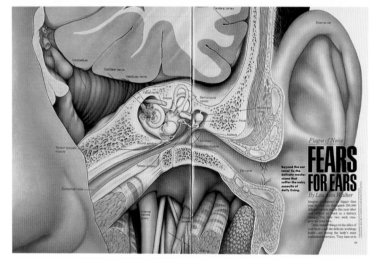

Publication **American Health**
Art Director **Will Hopkins**
Designers **Will Hopkins, Ira Friedlander**
Illustrators **Will Hopkins, Ira Friedlander**
Illustration Editor **Frank Kennard**
Photo Editor **Linda Eger**
Publisher **American Health Partners**
Agency **Will Hopkins Group**
Category **Single Page / Spread**
Date **January / Febraury 1987**

Publication **Conde Nast's Traveler**
Art Director **Lloyd Ziff**
Designer **Lloyd Ziff**
Photographer **Lloyd Ziff**
Photo Editor **Kathleen Klech**
Publisher **Conde Nast Publications, Inc.**
Category **Single Page / Spread**
Date **September 1987**

Publication **M.D. Practice**
Art Directors **Richard Kilmer, Mark Geer**
Designer **Mark Geer**
Illustrator **Matt Mahurin**
Client **Hermann Hospital**
Agency **Kilmer / Geer Design**
Category **Single Page / Spread**
Date **November 20, 1987**

Publication **American Country**
Art Directors **Will Hopkins, Ira Friedlander**
Designer **John Baxter**
Photographer **Marvin Newman**
Client **Mother Earth News Partners**
Agency **Will Hopkins Group**
Category **Single Page / Spread**
Date **July 1987**

Publication **M.D.**
Art Director **Merrill Cason**
Designer **Merrill Cason**
Photographer **Heeneg / Jackson**
Publisher **M.D. Publications**
Category **Single Page / Spread**
Date **April 1987**

Publication **Science Illustrated**
Art Director **John Isely**
Designer **John Isely**
Photographer **Bill Denison**
Publisher **Science Illustrated**
Category **Single Page / Spread**
Date **April / May 1987**

Publication **Time**
Art Director **Rudy Hoglund**
Designer **Nigel Holmes**
Publisher **Time, Inc.**
Category **Single Page / Spread**
Date **October 26, 1987**

Publication **Consumer Electronics Monthly**
Art Director **David Armario**
Designer **David Armario**
Illustrator **Jamie Bennett**
Publisher **International Thomson Publishers**
Category **Single Page / Spread**
Date **January 1987**

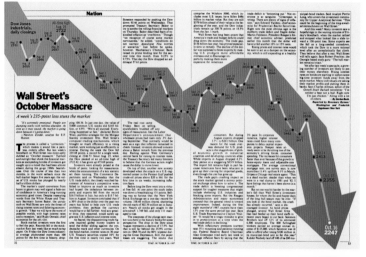

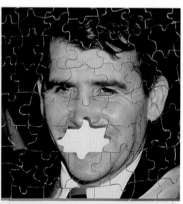

Publication **Time**
Art Director **Rudy Hoglund**
Designer **Arthur Hochstein**
Illustrator **Ed Sclafani**
Photographer **Ulf Skogsbergh**
Publisher **Time, Inc.**
Category **Single Page / Spread**
Date **July 13, 1987**

Publication **Consumer Electronics Monthly**
Art Director **David Armario**
Designer **David Armario**
Illustrator **Peter De Seve**
Publisher **International Thomson Publishers**
Category **Single Page / Spread**
Date **April 1987**

## Return to OZ

Tie me bustle bow down mate! With one foot planted in Australia's past and the other stepping lively into the future, top Aussie designers surface from down under with clothes that combine a wistful romance with modern style. On the upside down side of the globe, where the seasons are reversed, SCENE goes to the outback for an advance look at spring.

*Clothes by Peter Morrissey and Leona Edmiston.*

*Dollina's polyester print dress with lace collar, about $110. Dollina available at Jarrings, Austin, Texas.*

*Makeup by Clinique. Matte Ivory Superpowder Translucent, cheeks emphasized with Super Coral Young Face Powder Blusher; eyes highlighted with Night and Day Light Basic Eye Trapholizer, Semi-Satin Soft-Pressed Eye Shadow and Superblock Supermascara; and lips defined by Perfect Warmth Lip Pencil and Glazed Penny Different Lipstick.*

**FUN**

S O THERE'S ONLY ONE QUESTION THAT'S HOT," WROTE COLE PORTER "WILL WE HAVE FUN OR NOT?" THERE'S ONLY ONE ANSWER–YES! IN THE TRADITION OF GOLDFISH SWALLOWING, VW PACKING AND WATER BALLOON THROWING, SCENE HAS A LAUGH SKIRTS MAY GO — SOME COMPEN DIUM OF PEOPLE, PLACES AND THINGS UP. THE MARKET MAY GO DOWN AND YOUR CAREER MAY GO NOWHERE, BUT YOU CAN ALWAYS HAVE FUN. A WACKY JOB, OYSTERS IN DEAUVILLE OR CRUISING SUNSET BOULEVARD IN A PINK CADILLAC ARE A FEW OF THE POSSIBILITIES IN SCENE'S WORLD OF FUN

THE NEW GLAMOR

## ! THAT'SA FASHION

When the shape grabs your eye and there's plenty of thigh, that'sa fashion. Call it Cut-up Couture or Couture, the Sequel. For fall, designers rework some time-tested ideas of fashion's old guard into spicy off-the-rack fare. In Milan, the keys are terrific shape, smart details and a dose of mischief.

*PHOTOGRAPHED BY ANDREW MARTIN STYLING BY ELENA VIRSILA MAKEUP BY ED MELA HAIR BY SAPO • ALL TOGETHER*

*Krizia Più's evening separates in cotton, rayon and metallic. Top, $510, and skirt, $525, at the Krizia Boutique, New York, Palm Beach and Beverly Hills.*

Publication **Scene**
Art Director **Edward Leida**
Designer **Edward Leida**
Publisher **Fairchild Publications**
Category **Single Page / Spread**
Date **September 1987**

Publication **Scene**
Art Director **Edward Leida**
Designers **Edward Leida, Kirby Rodriguez**
Photographer **James Brill**
Publisher **Fairchild Publications**
Category **Single Page / Spread**
Date **December 1987**

Publication **Scene**
Art Director **Edward Leida**
Designer **Edward Leida**
Photographer **Andrew Martin**
Publisher **Fairchild Publications**
Category **Single Page / Spread**
Date **September 1987**

Publication **Enterprise**
Art Director **Ronn Campisi**
Designer **Ronn Campisi**
Illustrator **Patrick Blackwell**
Client **Digital Equipment Corporation**
Agency **Ronn Campisi Design**
Category **Single Page / Spread**
Date **Fall 1987**

Publication **Enterprise**
Art Director **Ronn Campisi**
Designer **Ronn Campisi**
Illustrator **Terry Widener**
Client **Digital Equipment Corporation**
Agency **Ronn Campisi Design**
Category **Single Page / Spread**
Date **Fall 1987**

Publication **Enterprise**
Art Director **John Howze**
Designer **John Howze**
Illustrator **Andrzej Dudzinski**
Client **Southwestern Bell Corporation**
Agency **Hawthorne / Wolfe Associates**
Category **Single Page / Spread**
Date **December 29, 1987**

78

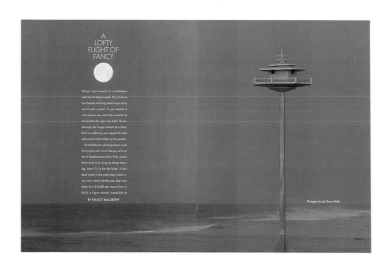

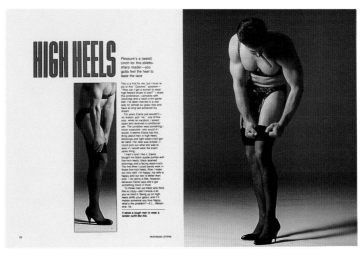

Publication **Almanac**
Art Director **Bridget De Socio**
Designer **Diane Kobar**
Photographer **Dana Hyde**
Client **Almanac Magazine**
Agency **Bridget De Socio**
Category **Single Page / Spread**
Date **September 1987**

Publication **Penthouse Letters**
Art Director **Danielle Gallo**
Designer **Laura Woods**
Photographer **Mitchel Gray**
Publisher **Penthouse International, Ltd.**
Category **Single Page / Spread**
Date **August 1987**

Publication **Mercedes**
Art Director **John Tom Cohoe**
Designer **John Tom Cohoe**
Photographer **Courtesy of Daimler Benz**
Client **Mercedes-Benz of North America**
Agency **McCaffrey-McCall**
Category **Single Page / Spread**
Date **July 1987**

Publication **Accessories**
Art Director **Hans Gschliesser**
Designer **Hans Gschliesser**
Photographers **Bill Morriss, Stephen Huszar**
Photo Editor **Irenka Jakubiak**
Publisher **Business Journals, Inc.**
Category **Single Page / Spread**
Date **October 1, 1987**

Publication **Warfields**
Art Director **Claude Skelton**
Designer **Claude Skelton**
Illustrator **Alan E. Cober**
Publisher **The Daily Record Co.**
Category **Single Page / Spread**
Date **June 1987**

Publication **Teen-Age Magazine**
Art Director **Robin Poosikian**
Designer **Robin Poosikian**
Photographer **George Lange / Outline Press**
Publisher **Computer Publishing Services, Inc.**
Category **Single Page / Spread**
Date **April / May 1987**

80

THE ESSENCE OF GRASSE

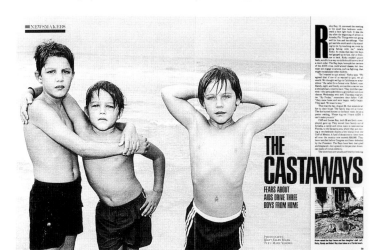

■NEWSMAKERS

THE CASTAWAYS

FEARS ABOUT
AIDS DRIVE THREE
BOYS FROM HOME

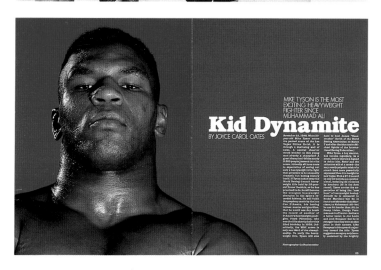

MIKE TYSON IS THE MOST
EXCITING HEAVYWEIGHT
FIGHTER SINCE
MUHAMMAD ALI

Kid Dynamite

BY JOYCE CAROL OATES

Publication **Life**
Art Director **Tom Bentkowski**
Designer **Robin Brown**
Photographer **Julio Donoso**
Publisher **Time, Inc.**
Category **Single Page / Spread**
Date **November 1987**

Publication **Life**
Art Director **Tom Bentkowski**
Designer **Nora Sheehan**
Photographer **Mary Ellen Mark**
Publisher **Time, Inc.**
Category **Single Page / Spread**
Date **October 1987**

Publication **Life**
Art Director **Charles Pates**
Designer **Nora Sheehan**
Photographer **Co Rentmeester**
Publisher **Time, Inc.**
Category **Single Page / Spread**
Date **March 1987**

Publication **Caring**
Art Director **Richard Kilmer**
Designer **Richard Kilmer**
Photographer **Michael Halloway**
Client **Memorial Care Systems**
Agency **Kilmer / Geer Design**
Category **Single Page / Spread**
Date **October 15, 1987**

Publication **Ambulatory Care**
Art Director **Scott Ray**
Designer **Scott Ray**
Illustrator **Bryan L. Peterson**
Client **National Association for Ambulatory Care**
Agency **Peterson & Company**
Category **Single Page / Spread**
Date **April 1987**

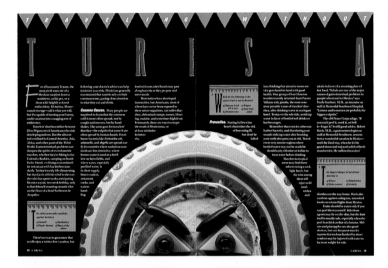

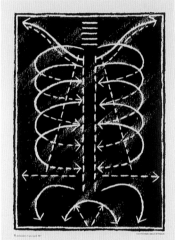

Publication **Building Profit**
Art Directors **William Hillenbrand, Keith Bollmer**
Designer **William Hillenbrand**
Client **Butler Manufacturing Inc.**
Agency **Wolf, Blumberg, Krody, Inc.**
Category **Single Page / Spread**
Date **Fall 1987**

Publication **Perspective**
Art Director **Joe McNeill**
Designer **David Loewy**
Illustrator **Brian Cronin**
Publisher **CMP Publications**
Category **Single Page / Spread**
Date **March 1987**

Publication **Metropolis**
Art Director **Helene Silverman**
Designer **Jeff Christensen**
Illustrator **Jeff Christensen**
Publisher **Metropolis Magazine**
Category **Single Page / Spread**
Date **November 1987**

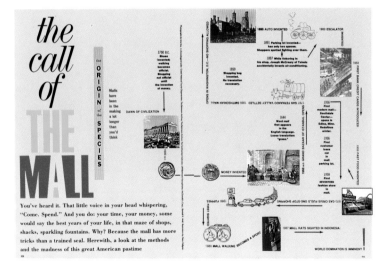

Publication **Seventeen**
Art Director **Melissa Warner**
Designer **Dania Martinez**
Illustrator **Gary Hallgren**
Publisher **Triangle Publications**
Category **Single Page / Spread**
Date **August 1987**

Publication **Stereo Review**
Art Director **Sue Llewellyn**
Designer **Sue Llewellyn**
Photographer **Hing / Norton**
Publisher **Diamandis Communications Inc.**
Category **Single Page / Spread**
Date **December 1987**

Publication **Sports Illustrated**
Art Director **Steven Hoffman**
Designer **Edward Truscio**
Photographer **Walter Iooss Jr.**
Publisher **Time, Inc.**
Category **Single Page / Spread**
Date **November 9, 1987**

Publication **Spirit of Audio**
Art Director **Miles Abernethy**
Designer **Miles Abernethy**
Photographer **Michael Sheperd**
Client **Audio of America, Inc.**
Agency **SHR Communications**
Category **Single Page / Spread**
Date **December 28, 1987**

Publication **M & D Journal**
Art Director **Beth Greely**
Photographer **Fred Collins**
Client **McCormack & Dodge**
Category **Single Page / Spread**
Date **November 15, 1987**

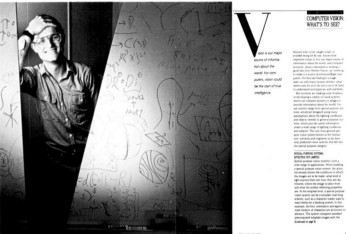

Publication **New Jersey Monthly**
Art Director **Nina Ovryn**
Designer **Barbara Walsh**
Photographer **Pete Byron**
Publisher **Micromedia Arts**
Category **Single Page / Spread**
Date **December 1987**

Publication **R.P. Magazine**
Art Director **John Howze**
Designer **John Howze**
Photographer **Richard Pedroncelli**
Photo Editor **John Howze / Keith Schopp**
Client **Ralston Purina Co.**
Agency **Hawthorne / Wolfe Assoc.**
Category **Single Page / Spread**
Date **May 15, 1987**

Publication **The Boston Globe**
Art Director **Aldona Charlton**
Designer **Aldona Charlton**
Photographer **Jan Houseworth, Globe**
Publisher **The Boston Globe**
Category **Single Page / Spread**
Date **January 30, 1987**

Publication **The Boston Globe / Travel Section**
Art Director **Richard M. Baker**
Designer **Richard M. Baker**
Illustrator **Marty Braun**
Publisher **The Boston Globe**
Category **Single Page / Spread**
Date **March 29, 1987**

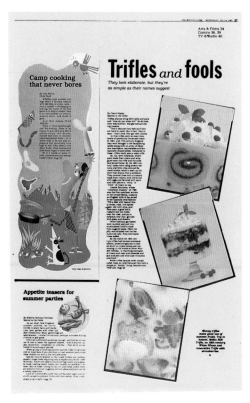

Publication **The Boston Globe**
Art Director **Lynn Staley**
Designer **Lynn Staley**
Publisher **The Boston Globe**
Category **Single Page / Spread**
Date **April 5, 1987**

Publication **The Boston Globe**
Art Director **Rena Sokolow**
Designer **Rena Sololow**
Illustrators **Terry Allen, Mark Falls**
Photographer **Ned McCormick**
Publisher **The Boston Globe**
Category **Single Page / Spread**
Date **July 8, 1987**

Publication **The Washington Post**
Art Director **Michael Keegan**
Designer **Carol Porter**
Illustrator **Jeff Dever**
Publisher **The Washington Post**
Category **Single Page / Spread**
Date **September 30, 1987**

Publication **The Wall Street Journal / Special Reports**
Art Director **Joe Dizney**
Designer **Joe Dizney**
Illustrator **Rosemary Webber**
Publisher **Dow Jones & Company, Inc.**
Category **Single Page / Spread**
Date **December 4, 1987**

Publication **The New York Times / Op-Ed**
Art Director **Jerelle Kraus**
Designer **Jerelle Kraus**
Illustrator **Brian Cronin**
Publisher **The New York Times**
Category **Single Page / Spread**
Date **July 4, 1987**

Publication **Florida**
Art Director **Santa Choplin**
Designer **Santa Choplin**
Illustrator **Val Tillery**
Publisher **The Orlando Sentinel**
Category **Single Page / Spread**
Date **October 18, 1987**

Publication **Elle**
Art Director **Phyllis Schefer**
Designer **Olivia Badrutt**
Photographer **Oliviero Toscani**
Publisher **Murdoch / Hachette**
Publication Director **Regis Pagniez**
Category **Story Presentation**
Date **September 1987**

Publication **Elle**
Art Director **Phyllis Schefer**
Designer **Phyllis Schefer**
Photographer **Marc Hispard**
Publisher **Murdoch / Hachette**
Publication Director **Regis Pagniez**
Category **Story Presentation**
Date **May 1987**

Publication **Elle**
Art Director **Phyllis Schefer**
Designer **Phyllis Schefer**
Photographer **Oliviero Toscani**
Publisher **Murdoch / Hachette**
Publication Director **Regis Pagniez**
Category **Story Presentation**
Date **April 1987**

Publication **Elle**
Art Director **Phyllis Schefer**
Designer **Regis Pagniez**
Photographer **Anne Pagniez**
Publisher **Murdoch / Hachette**
Publication Director **Regis Pagniez**
Category **Story Presentation**
Date **May 1987**

Publication **Conde Nast's Traveler**
Art Director **Lloyd Ziff**
Designer **Lloyd Ziff**
Photographer **Herb Ritts**
Photo Editor **Kathleen Klech**
Publisher **Conde Nast Publications, Inc.**
Category **Story Presentation**
Date **November 1987**

# THE CARIBB EAN REPORT

THE GREAT BEACH FINDER:
The definitive guide to thirty island beaches
THE ROCKRESORTS:
What's happened to the millionaire's dream?
PLUS:
The experts choose the
best resorts, golf, and music

PHOTOGRAPHED BY HERB RITTS

**90**

THE CARIBBEAN REPORT: SAND AND WATER
The dream encountered: Solitude on St. Barts

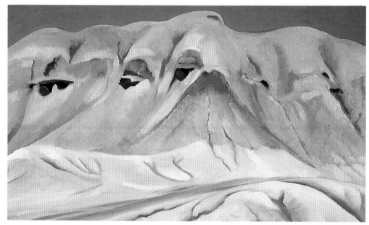

Publication **Conde Nast's Traveler**
Art Director **Lloyd Ziff**
Designer **Lloyd Ziff**
Photographers **Juan Hamilton, Macco Varon**
Photo Editor **Kathleen Klech**
Publisher **Conde Nast Publications, Inc.**
Category **Story Presentation**
Date **November 1987**

Publication **Connoisseur**
Art Director **Sandra Di Pasqua**
Designer **Sandra Di Pasqua**
Photographer **William Wegman**
Photo Editor **Phyllis Levine**
Publisher **The Hearst Corporation**
Category **Story Presentation**
Date **November 1987**

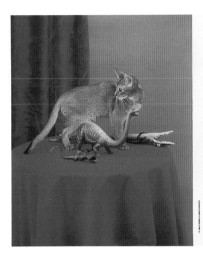

*G*old-green eyes alert to danger, sleek body primed for attack.

*A*byssinians remain wild, capricious, and provocative all their lives.

*O*ne is born an Abyssinian (person) or not. It is not something one grows into.

WILL AN ABY CHANGE YOUR LIFE?

Publication **House and Garden**
Art Director **Karen Lee Grant**
Designer **Karen Lee Grant**
Photographers **Collection of William McCarty Cooper,**
**Kunsh Museum, Basel, Switzerland**
Photo Editor **Tom McWilliam**
Publisher **Conde Nast Publications, Inc.**
Category **Story Presentation**
Date **October 1987**

**92**

# PICASSO'S SECRET LOVE

BY JOHN RICHARDSON

Despite all that has been written about Picasso, there are still vast gaps in our knowledge of his life. Certain things the artist chose to keep dark, others he contrived to forget, and like many great men he came to believe his own legends. One episode he chose to forget was his passionate love affair in 1915–16 with an unknown Parisienne, Gaby Lespinasse. Apart from a brief mention by Pierre Daix of a mysterious "Madame L," nothing has been recorded of this ravishing girl whom Picasso kept a secret from even his closest friends, not least Gertrude Stein and Alice Toklas. Witness their account (in the former's

Gaby Lespinasse, opposite, often photographed, possibly by Picasso, 1915–16. Opposite left: His geometric watercolor designs of 1916. Left: Nude study of Gaby Lespinasse, pencil, early 1916, private collection. One of a series of drawings the artist put on the market in the late 1950s after closing the compromising inscriptions. Above: Photograph of Picasso, c. 1915

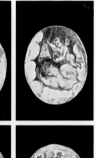

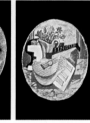

where he has been one of the earliest settlers.

Not the least of the mysteries raised by Gaby's little treasure trove is the whereabouts of the rooms depicted in these watercolors—rooms that evidently had very special memories for the artist, given the tenderness that imbues them. The Provençal rusticity could hardly be less Parisian, nor does it correspond to the look of either of Picasso's Parisian abodes in 1916: the studio on the rue Schoelcher or the little house at Montrouge. The tiled floor *(cimetières de Marseille, if I am not wrong), the earthenware pots, the rush chairs, the Provençal bahuts (chests), the bundle of carments de sope (faggots made of vine prunings), and the open fireplace with the cooking pot on the hob would indicate the Midi, the south of France. The Mediterranean, one feels, is not too far away, and one can almost smell the lavender and rosemary outside the window. True, there is no record in the literature of the artist's leaving Paris in the course of 1916, but isn't it only too likely he would have abandoned the death-haunted capital for a spring or summer vacation in the south, as he had done in the past and would do again and again in the future? (Text continued on page 292)*

Gaby Lespinasse, below, 1915–16. Right: Gaby's memorabilia of her romance with Picasso: photographs of the two, a declaration of love, and a prayer to God for her hand in marriage. Opposite: Three still lifes and a portrait of Gaby with a cherub.

The artist with his guard down, passionately, abjectly in love, for once at the mercy of a pretty girl instead of the other way around

groups *The Autobiography of Alice B. Toklas)* of a visit in 1916 to Picasso's little house in that dismal Parisian suburb Montrouge. They found him very cheerful, but the only girlfriends they identify are "Paquerette a girl who was very nice [and] Irene a very lovely woman who came from the mountains and wanted to be free

Why no mention of Gaby Lespinasse, his principal love of this period? Because nobody—not even Stein or Toklas—had been vouchsafed a glimpse of her. Picasso was often secretive and jealous where his mistresses were concerned, and he had a pasha's tendency to lock them away, above all from predators men and even women. There were other excellent reasons for keeping this romance secret. Gaby, it seems, was already involved with the American-born engraver and poet Herbert Lespinasse, whom she would eventually marry, at least she had adopted his name. We also have to bear in mind the discreditable fact that the romance began sometime in the fall of 1915, when the artist was supposed to be inconsolable because tuberculosis was about to carry off his current mistress, the frail and beautiful Eva Gouel (Picasso had symbolically changed her name from Marcelle to Eva, "the first woman," he said, thus implying that he was the first man). He let her waft too ready to be consoled. Ever since his younger sister, Conchita, had died of diphtheria twenty years earlier, Picasso had suffered from a guilty fear of disease and mortality, and in order to generate the courage to hold Eva's hand, as he dutifully did every day while she faded away in a clinic the other side of Paris at Auteuil, he needed someone to hold his hand. Bear in mind, too, that for Picasso guilt acted as an aphrodisiac. And so he embarked on a passionate affair with a girl who was as gentle and sweet and vulnerable as the one who was dying

Picasso's *The Montlié Bedroom*, opposite, watercolor, 1916. Above left: Another watercolor of Gaby Lespinasse, early 1916. The artist preferred to portray his beautiful mistress in profile. He painted each of the 16 wooden beads of his necklace for Gaby with a different pattern. Left: Even Picasso's plea that Gaby should come back to him took a decorative form.

Gaby's independence explains Picasso's insistent cajolery

REVIENS MON
AMOUR
Boss MON ANGE

The *Provençal Kitchen* ends with a characteristically Picassian conceit—*Je t'aime de toutes les couleurs,* the words *Je t'aime* reiterated in six different colors

A quaint device that recurs is his name entwined with hers— calligraphic lovemaking

Publication **Metropolitan Home**
Art Director **Don Morris**
Designer **Richard Ferretti**
Publisher **Meredith Corporation**
Category **Story Presentation**
Date **April 1987**

Publication **The Boston Globe Magazine**
Art Director **Lucy Bartholomay**
Designer **Lucy Bartholomay**
Illustrator **Ken Maryianski**
Publisher **The Boston Globe**
Category **Single Page / Spread**
Date **November 29, 1987**

Publication **The Boston Globe Magazine**
Art Director **Gail Anderson**
Designer **Gail Anderson**
Illustrator **Vivienne Flesher**
Publisher **The Boston Globe**
Category **Single Page / Spread**
Date **April 15, 1987**

94

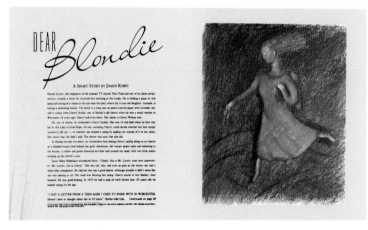

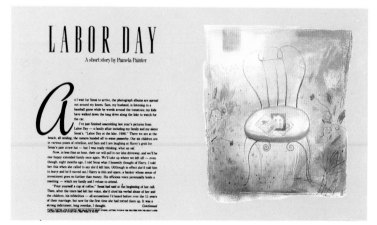

Publication **The Boston Globe Magazine**
Art Director **Lucy Bartholomay**
Designer **Lucy Bartholomay**
Illustrator **Seth Jaben**
Publisher **The Boston Globe**
Category **Single Page / Spread**
Date **October 18, 1987**

Publication **The Boston Globe Magazine**
Art Director **Lucy Bartholomay**
Designer **Lucy Bartholomay**
Illustrator **Regan Dunnick**
Publisher **The Boston Globe**
Category **Single Page / Spread**
Date **November 8, 1987**

Publication **The Boston Globe Magazine**
Art Director **Gail Anderson**
Designer **Gail Anderson**
Illustrator **Vivienne Flesher**
Publisher **The Boston Globe**
Category **Single Page / Spread**
Date **August 30, 1987**

Publication **Life**
Art Director **Charles W. Pates**
Designer **Robin Brown**
Publisher **Time, Inc.**
Category **Story Presentation**
Date **March 1987**

Publication **Life**
Art Director **Tom Bentkowski**
Designer **Tom Bentkowski**
Photographer **Denis Waugh**
Publisher **Time, Inc.**
Category **Story Presentation**
Date **October 1987**

Publication **Life**
Art Director **Tom Bentkowski**
Designer **Tom Bentkowski**
Photographer **Mary Ellen Mark**
Publisher **Time, Inc.**
Category **Story Presentation**
Date **December 1987**

# A WEEK IN THE LIFE OF A HOMELESS FAMILY

# CHILD OF SILENCE

RETRIEVED FROM THE SHADOW-WORLD OF AUTISM, KATY FINDS HER VOICE

Publication **Life**
Art Director **Charles W. Pates**
Designer **Nora Sheehan**
Photographer **Mary Ellen Mark**
Publisher **Time, Inc.**
Category **Story Presentation**
Date **September 1987**

Publication **Life**
Art Director **Tom Bentkowski**
Designer **Tom Bentkowski**
Photographer **Enrico Ferorre III**
Publisher **Time, Inc.**
Category **Story Presentation**
Date **October 1987**

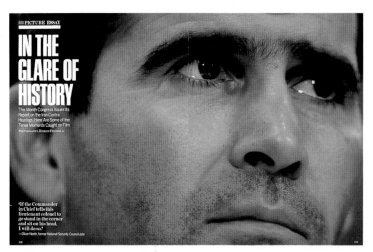

PICTURE ESSAY

# IN THE GLARE OF HISTORY

This Month Congress Issues Its
Report on the Iran-Contra
Hearings. Here Are Some of the
Tense Moments Caught on Film
PHOTOGRAPHS: ENRICO FERORELLI

'If the Commander
in Chief tells this
lieutenant colonel to
go stand in the corner
and sit on his head,
I will do so.'
—Oliver North, former National Security Council aide

'The President was astonished. His jaw
set, and his eyes flashed. I finally felt
that the President deeply understands
something is radically wrong.'
—George Shultz, secretary of state

'I just didn't think
it would work, and
I was against the
whole policy.'
—Caspar Weinberger, secretary of defense

'I made a very
deliberate decision
not to ask the
President so
that I could
insulate him....'
—John Poindexter, former
national security adviser

'I was careful not to
ask Colonel North
questions I did not
need the answers to.'
—Elliott Abrams, assistant secretary of state

'Colonel, there's
a saying that
failure is
an orphan.'
—Arthur Liman, chief counsel for the Senate, to Oliver North

Publication **Milwaukee**
Art Directors **Sharon Nelson, Victoria Vaccarello**
Designers **Sharon Nelson, Victoria Vaccarello**
Publisher **Milwaukee Magazine**
Category **Story Presentation**
Date **August 1987**

## Designing the
# AMERICAN DREAM

Decades ago, housewives swooned over shapely pastel appliances while husbands yearned for streamlined Studebakers and Lawn-Boy mowers. They were some of the everyday innovations marking America's transition to a full-blown consumer society. And they were some of the things for which Milwaukee's Brooks Stevens has never gotten quite enough credit.

BY PERRY M. LAMEK

# L●CATION!
# L●CATION!
# L●CATION!

The Japanese have set their sights on
Washington real estate · By Harry Jaffe

Publication **Regardie's**
Art Director **Fred Woodward**
Designer **Fred Woodward**
Photographer **Jim Meyers**
Publisher **Regardie's**
Category **Story Presentation**

Publication **Regardie's**
Art Director **Fred Woodward**
Designer **Jolene Cuyler**
Photographer **Kent Barker**
Publisher **Regardie's**
Category **Story Presentation**
Date **April 1987**

In a town that fancies
itself Mount Olympus, somebody has to play the part of Mercury

# MESSENGERS

## OF THE GODS

*Photography*

KENT BARKER

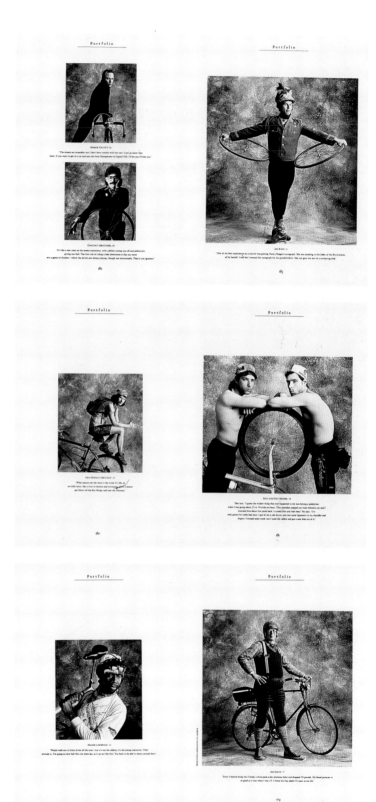

Publication **Rolling Stone**
Art Director **Fred Woodward**
Designer **Fred Woodward**
Publisher **Straight Arrow Publishers**
Category **Story Presentation and Single Issue**
Date **December 17-31, 1987**

**100**

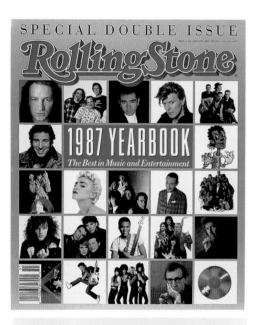

In 1987, planes, portfolios and politicians crashed in alarming numbers. Yuppies were forced to abandon their greed-crazed climb to the top, while a presidential candidate and a TV evangelist slept their way to the bottom.

# THE YEAR THAT FELL TO EARTH

## By P.J. O'Rourke

THE BIMBO, A SPECIES thought extinct for more than twenty years, resurfaced with a vengeance in 1987. A bimbo is a young woman who's not pretty enough to be a model, not smart enough to be an actress and not nice enough to be a poisonous snake. The woods were full of them – political bimbo Donna Rice, fundamentalist bimbo Jessica Hahn, arms-deal bimbo Fawn Hall and all-purpose bimbo maximo Vanna White. There were even Russian bimbos, seducing U.S. Marine embassy guards with large, lumpy but nonetheless tantalizing Soviet-style sexual favors. In the bimbo senior division, First Lady Nancy Reagan wretched her husband's White House staff, and former Miss America Bess Myerson allegedly suborned a divorce-court judge on behalf of her scumbo boyfriend.

Some readers may condemn the paragraph above for sexism – and they're right. But before the boys in the audience get too smug, maybe we should consider who the real bimbos are. Ronald Reagan, for example, has made it all the way to the highest office in the world on the basis of his looks. Ollie North almost got away with deserving America's foreign policy because of his dizzy cuteness and chestful of pretty medals. And Jim Bakker – Sure, his wife, Tammy Faye wore lots of makeup, cried on TV and bamboozled the public, but Jim tried to pull the same things on God. In the bimbo profession, as in every other, women still lack equal opportunity.

The bimbos of 1987 changed the course of American politics, plunged the U.S. into a theological crisis, brought us one step closer to war in Central America, compromised our national security and caused an economically troubled nation to waste millions of precious man-hours on moronic TV game shows.

In a related development, the women's movement quietly died. The meaning mistaken came back. The Schneider ended her presidential campaign in girlish tears. And Ms. magazine (whose cofounder, Gloria Steinem, now

**DONNA, FAWN AND JESSICA** *by Anita Kunz*

"The beach before [the sirens] is piled with bondheaps of men now rotted away." – THE ODYSSEY

ROLLING STONE · 123

---

darts loathsome real-estate parents Mortthan Zuckerman) was sold to an Australian publishing firm. Rerun has a that the first 86. state under new management still feature a cover story titled "What Every Free Dream Media Should Know About Keeping To Digest's Stare Gold."

**Personal computer** sales were up again in time for personal computer users to discover that eight percent of all the people who own personal computers just lose everything in the stock market.

**A number of stock** market readers went over to yours and – considering what happened to stocks – were darn glad to be there.

**Also get a** lot of trouble for using the Beatles "Revolution" as theme music for a sneaker commercial. The company apologized, saying it had intended to use "Kill the Poor" by the Dead Kennedys, but had not even technical problems due to some recent remarks.

**A girls with Gary Hart** nearly ruined the career of promising young pharmaceutical salesperson Donna Rice. Hart then lost his chance to become president of the United States by guessing wrong when asked by a member of the conventional press, "Have you ever committed adultery?"

The correct answer to that question is "Yeah, twice, once with and once another." Political analysts agree that seemingly untruthful Mr. Hartpence would have been made pres by acclaim had he said the truth.

**The Saudi Arabians** killed hundreds of non-ing Iranian Shrews during the annual pilgrimage to the holy city of Mecca, causing a global outpouring of sympathy and concern such as has not been seen since Ivan Boesky was sentenced for insider trading.

**The 200th anniversary** of the U.S. Constitution was celebrated. Everyone believes the document needs some modifications. Foremost among these is a change in the First Amendment so that it cannot everybody but Howard Stern.

**A Japanese insurance** company paid the largest amount ever for a painting, "Van Gogh's Sunflowers." The price was $39.9 million, which at the current exchange rate is about 35 yen.

**The United States** and the Soviet Union have nearly concluded a pact eliminating short- and medium-range weapons from their nuclear arsenals. The new treaty will ensure that when World War III breaks out, everyone will have at least twenty minutes to talk to and phone friends.

**THE PIT BULL** *by Everett Peck*
Team '87

**JIM AND TAMMY BAKKER** *by C.F. Payne*

"It cannot serve God and mammon."

124 · ROLLING STONE, DECEMBER 17TH – DECEMBER 31ST, 1987

ROLLING STONE · 125

---

leading citizen biologists to support that presidential candidates have been sentencing to the Atlantic.

**The Federal Communications Commission** has rescinded the famous doctrine. Presidential candidates can now say their opponents are lying like gerbils without TV networks being required to offer the small stations equal time.

**Bono-brain wording** of incestual voters at the 1988 Democratic presidential primaries found Jesse Jackson running second to "Fuck you, get off my lunch!" Jackson's presidential campaign has prompted an unusual rash of death threats. More than 500 career Democrats have vowed to kill anybody who does anything to damage Jackson's candidacy.

**The smart money** in Massachusetts governor Michael Dukakis for the 1988 Democratic presidential nomination. The Duke's wife used to be pulled, not shapes on-sprayed, but campaign managers agreed on Joe Biden, the state where he's governor is famous for high taxes, municipal corruption, bad racial attitudes and shocking pink political ads. So Dukakis does look pretty good compared with the rest of the Dems hopefuls. But for for a ticket-balancing step, choose a conservative Southern black woman who's strong on national defense. (Please call Democratic party headquarters in Washington ASAP if you know anyone answering this description.)

**Republican candidate** Bob Dole and Jack Kemp were reaching hard to rise as big a stem on the campaign trail as George Bush. "That's one thing about Republicans," said a Dole campaign aide. "You sure there to get them sleep. Otherwise, they get grumpy and go even fire a George Walker or something."

**Prostitution of bored** as defenses by Marilyn Hart as a single engine Cessna and deliver all the whole Libyan army by Cleobatra driving Toyota packing trucks seemed to indicate the U.S. will wage the secret-making missions, crackpot war-tech analog turns to be sine assert. Americans have already shown a remarkable ability to kill people while using such simple technology as hardpigeon, illegal drugs and driving while drunk. Since the American's armed forces already have handguns, it's legal drugs and drunks to ample supply, without leaving would be on it easy.

**OLIVER NORTH** *by Philip Burke*

"Beau and Mosjus Frames"

**BRIGITTE AND SLY, PETER AND JOAN** *by Robert Risko*

"Sick Buggers of 1987"

150 · ROLLING STONE, DECEMBER 17TH – DECEMBER 31ST, 1987

ROLLING STONE · 151

---

between them. The unprecedented surgical procedure raised medical hopes for Ron and Nancy Reagan.

**A new batch of words,** easy stand-up comedians took America by storm – Bob Goldthwait, Sam Kinison, Dana Plato. Most popular by far was a mincelytoned Puddi-Kutt performer who teamed America to a disco feeling as all too clear loving sex and using condoms. To gotta love that laugh out Julie Paid D – what a funny, manic, crazy guy!

**Hey, where's all the stock** go? In 1986 the stuff was all over the place, threatening health and well-being on every front. And the stuff disappear. Where is it anyway? In 1986 the...

**A soft styled "potato rock clothes"** all the court of Long Island was found by the FCC. "We had to do it," said an FCC spokesman. "They'd played Jimmy Buffett's 'Son of a Son of a Sailor' thirty-nine times in a row."

A veteran manager defended his plaudits. "There really isn't all that much power rock to choose from," he said. "I mean, there's that horrible Christopher Cross song. And then there's a bunch of old cocaine that doesn't a bunch of old cocaine chance can't be find less. We're sorry. We just didn't know what else to play."

**August 16th was** the date on "harmonic convergence." Three important planets lined up with a new moon. Nothing horrible happened. This was the only time during 1987 when nothing horrible did. Obviously there's something to this harmonic convergence stuff.

**A complete list** of all the good news is:
• After unflagged as an American vessel, the Kuwaiti oil tanker Liars Al-Andi had its name changed to Joe? or.
• Prominent anthropologist Solomon Katz announced the theory that all civilization began with beer.
• The U.S. and Canada signed a free-trade pact that will vastly decrease the cost of Eskimo sunglasses art and plaid flannel lots with cardigan.
• MTV ownership is off.
• The cellular-phone industry has greatly expanded, making complete to sit and long-distance service available to the homeless.
• These useful million-main pro priorities declined in popularity.
• The national speed limit was increased to sixty-five (although nearly in parts of the country where there isn't anywhere to go).
• The Ollie North doll was not in commercial success.

**A mysterious bright** die-off along the East Coast was blamed on politicians.

**YUPPIES FLEE WALL STREET** *by Steven Guarnaccia*

"If I can make it there, I'll make it anywhere." – NEW YORK, NEW YORK

**RONALD REAGAN** *by Steven Pietzsch*

"Pay no attention to the man behind that curtain." – THE WIZARD OF OZ

128 · ROLLING STONE, DECEMBER 17TH – DECEMBER 31ST, 1987

ROLLING STONE · 129

> NEW FACES <

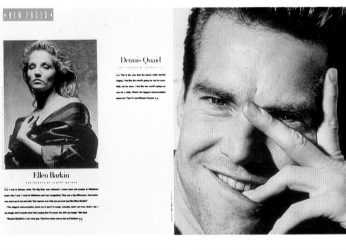

**Ellen Barkin**
PHOTOGRAPH BY ALBERT WATSON

**Dennis Quaid**
PHOTOGRAPH BY HERB RITTS

> NEW FACES <

**Robert Cray**
PHOTOGRAPH BY LARA ROSSIGNOL

**Suzanne Vega**
PHOTOGRAPH BY DOUGLAS BRIAN

> NEW FACES <

**Blair Brown**
PHOTOGRAPH BY LOU SCIARENCI

**Robert Townsend**
PHOTOGRAPH BY MARK HANAUER

> NEW FACES <

**Kevin Costner**
PHOTOGRAPH BY HERB RITTS

**Holly Hunter**
PHOTOGRAPH BY GEORGE HOLZ

Publication **Rolling Stone**
Art Director **Fred Woodward**
Designer **Fred Woodward**
Photo Editor **Laurie Kratochvil**
Publisher **Straight Arrow Publishers**
Category **Story Presentation**
Date **December 17-31, 1987**

Publication **Texas Monthly**
Art Director **D.J. Stout**
Designer **D.J. Stout**
Photographers **William Coupon, Kent Barker**
Photo Editor **D.J. Stout**
Publisher **Texas Monthly**
Category **Story Presentation**
Date **November 1987**

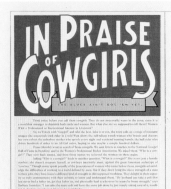

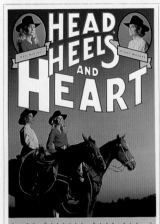

Publication **Texas Monthly**
Art Director **D.J. Stout**
Designer **D.J. Stout**
Photographer **Tom Ryan**
Publisher **Texas Monthly**
Category **Story Presentation**
Date **August 1987**

Publication **Rolling Stone**
Art Director **Fred Woodward**
Designer **Jolene Cuyler**
Photographer **Matthew Rolston**
Photo Editor **Laurie Kratochvil**
Publisher **Straight Arrow Publishers**
Category **Story Presentation**
Date **January 28, 1987**

# GEORGE MICHAEL, SERIOUSLY

*Wham! was something of a joke, but now Michael has made a brilliant solo debut,* **AND** *no one's laughing anymore* **BY STEVE POND**

PHOTOGRAPHS BY MATTHEW ROLSTON

104

# Epilogue for TITANIC

By ROBERT D. BALLARD

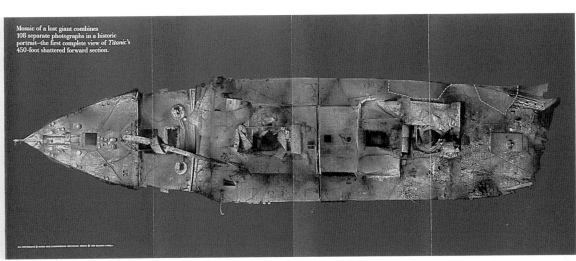

Mosaic of a lost giant combines 108 separate photographs in a historic portrait—the first complete view of *Titanic*'s 450-foot shattered forward section.

## How the unsinkable ship sank

Robert Ballard's hope that *Titanic* should remain undisturbed was not realized. Last July, a French expedition began to retrieve artifacts from the wreck site. Its actions were roundly criticized as grave robbing—justifiably, for the line between curiosity and acquisitiveness seems to have been crossed.

—THE EDITOR

Publication **National Geographic**

Art Director **Jan Adkins**

Designer **Gerard A. Valerio**

Illustrators **W.M. Bond, Ken Marschall**

Photographer **Robert Ballard**

Photo Editor **Bob Hernandez**

Publisher **National Geographic Society**

Category **Story Presentation**

Date **October 1987**

Publication **The Washington Post Magazine**
Art Director **Brian Noyes**
Designer **Brian Noyes**
Illustrator **Stan Watts, Brian Noyes**
Photographer **Molly Roberts**
Publisher **The Washington Post**
Category **Story Presentation**
Date **July 5, 1987**

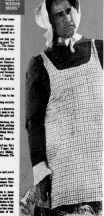

Publication **Premiere**
Art Directors **David Walters, Robert Best**
Designer **David Walters**
Photographer **G. Rancinan, Fabian**
Publisher **Murdoch / Hachette**
Category **Story Presentation**
Date **November 1987**

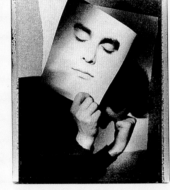

First it was no salt and no caffeine. Then no smoking, please. Then it was time to say no to drugs. Then there was herpes, and now there's AIDS, so it's no to sex. Add it all up and you've got . . .

by David Seeley

## The NO Decade

*Like a lot of people, I have been pushed too far. It's as of some serious conspiracy is trying to make us behave. Being told what not to do at every turn robs us of our right to choose. This is why, that night, I felt trapped.*

Publication **Texas Monthly**
Art Director **D.J. Stout**
Designer **D.J. Stout**
Photographer **Geof Kern**
Photo Editor **D.J. Stout**
Publisher **Texas Monthly**
Category **Story Presentation**
Date **June 1987**

Publication **Homes International**
Art Director **Alice Cooke**
Designer **Alice Cooke**
Publisher / Client **Coldwell Banker**
Category **Story Presentation**
Date **September 1987**

The Private Islands of the Caribbean

T
hey could be called the special islands of the Caribbean. However, they are so secluded, and so separate, that these unknown hideaways in the sea of personal sun could be anywhere. Their names are unknown to all but a select few, who have been fortunate enough to visit them, or have heard about them from friends, or perhaps have caught them on such television programs as "Life Styles of the Rich and Famous." Yet, they are fast becoming the preeminent warm weather destinations for upscale travelers from everywhere around the world.

By Stanley H. Murray

The resort-shaped secluded beach at Guana Island, with the mountains in the background.

J

L

Publication **Architecture Minnesota**
Art Director **Jim Cordaro**
Designer **Jim Cordaro**
Photographer **David Husom**
Publisher **Institute of American Architecture**
Agency **Rubin / Cordaro Design**
Category **Story Presentation**
Date **January / February 1987**

## DIGESTIVE UPSETS

They won't kill you, but they can sure make your life miserable. Here's how to keep them from getting the best of you and recognize trouble when it's on the way.

---

### MADE IN MINNESOTA

# COUNTY FAIRGROUNDS

Sometimes on the edge of town, sometimes in the country, the 86 county fairgrounds of Minnesota form a ready-made collection of common buildings. Heart and soul were put into these simple structures and, though one would be hard-pressed to identify a distinct vocabulary for each county, the fairgrounds do speak with local accents. In Grand Marais on Lake Superior's north shore, it is the dialect of the Scandinavian cabin. In New Ulm, the German brogue of the stepped brick pattern. In Aitkin and Mahnomen, the flat tones of the honest farmer. All speak plainly and with a certain native wit. *Photography by David Husom.*

Traverse County
Wheaton

Aitkin County
Aitkin

Todd County
Long Prairie

St. Louis County
Hibbing

Brown County
New Ulm

Wright County
Howard Lake

Pine County
Pine City

Aitkin County
Aitkin

Cook County
Grand Marais

Mahnomen County
Mahnomen

Publication **Caring**
Art Director **Mark Geer**
Designer **Mark Geer**
Illustrator **Cathie Bleck**
Publisher **Memorial Care Systems**
Agency **Kilmer / Geer Design**
Category **Story Presentation**
Date **October 15, 1987**

Publication **Sacramento Bee**
Art Director **James Carr**
Designer **James Carr**
Photographer **Genaro Molina**
Photo Editor **George Wedding**
Publisher **The Sacramento Bee Magazine**
Category **Story Presentation**
Date **August 30, 1987**

110

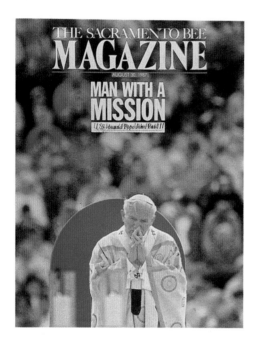

"VIVA IL PAPA!"

PRAYERFUL AND POWERFUL, JOHN PAUL II IS EQUALLY AT HOME IN THE SPIRITUAL AND TEMPORAL WORLDS.

"VIVA IL PAPA!"

FROM LOLLIPOPS TO LOTTERIES, PEOPLE ARE PROFITING FROM THE IMAGE OF THE HOLY FATHER.

"VIVA IL PAPA!"

KAROL WOJTYLA HAS TOUCHED THE LIVES OF MORE CATHOLICS THAN ANY OTHER PONTIFF.

Publication **The New York Times Magazine**
Art Director **Diana LaGuardia**
Designer **Audrone Razgaitis**
Publisher **The New York Times**
Category **Story Presentation**
Date **October 4, 1987**

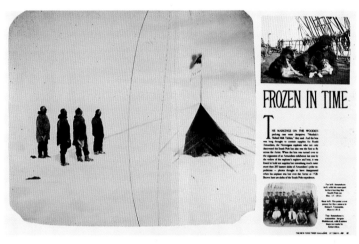

Publication **The New York Times Magazine**
Art Director **Diana LaGuardia**
Designer **Janet Froelich**
Illustrator **Eugene Mihaesco**
Publisher **The New York Times**
Category **Story Presentation**
Date **April 5, 1987**

Publication **Artforum**
Art Director **Tibor Kalman**
Designer **Emily Oberman**
Client **Artforum**
Agency **M & Co.**
Category **Single Issue**
Date **October 1987**

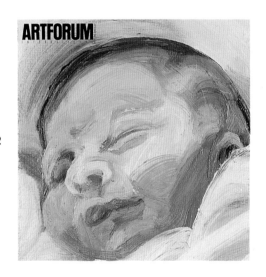

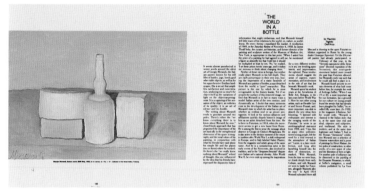

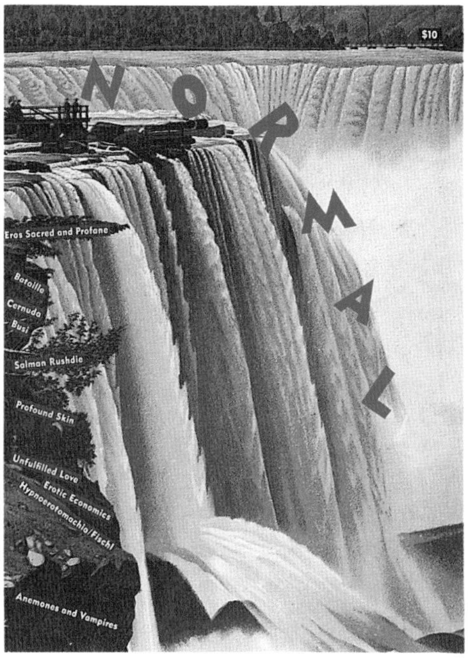

$10
NORMAL
Eros Sacred and Profane
Bataille
Cernuda
Busi
Salman Rushdie
Profound Skin
Unfulfilled Love
Erotic Economics
Hypnoerotomachia/Fischl
Anemones and Vampires


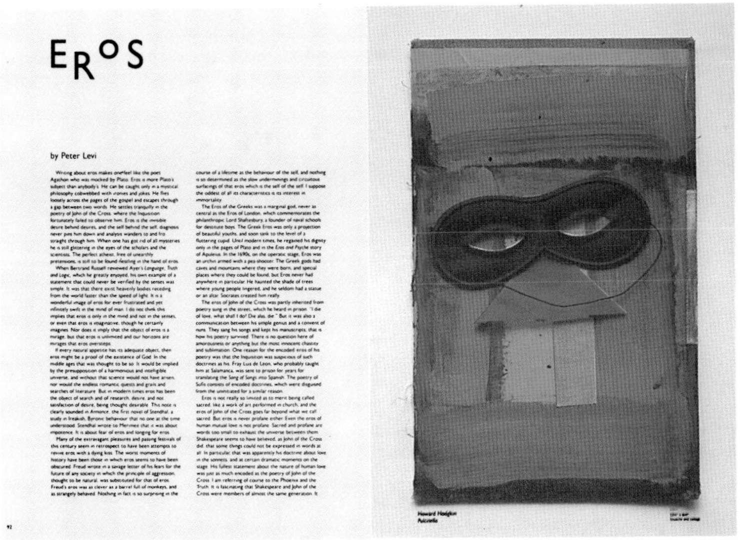

EROS
by Peter Levi


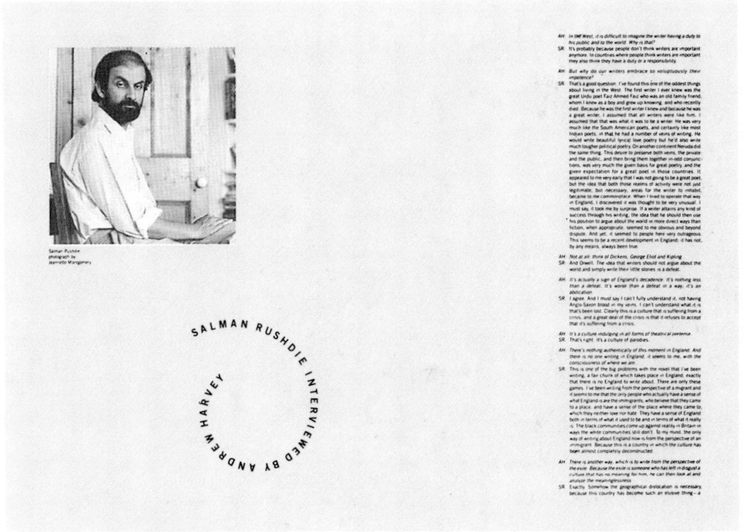

SALMAN RUSHDIE INTERVIEWED BY ANDREW HARVEY


113

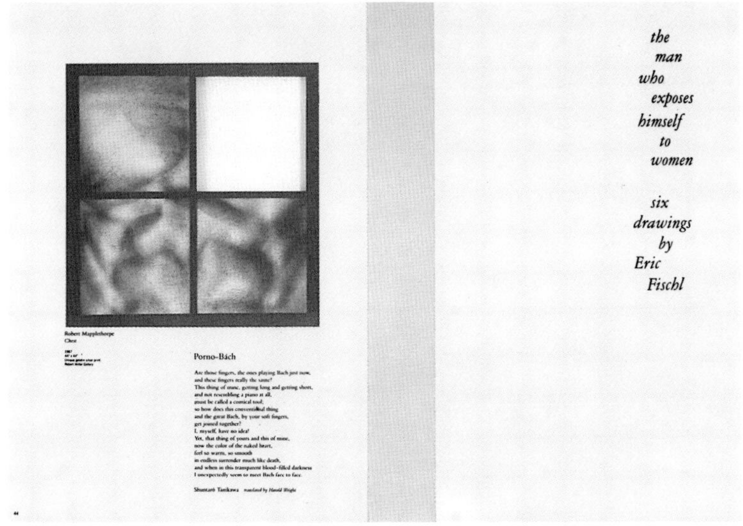

the man who exposes himself to women
six drawings by Eric Fischl
Porno-Bach


Publication **Normal 2**
Art Director **Paul Davis**
Designers **Jose Conde, Jeanine Esposito**
Illustrator **Robert Mapplethorpe**
Publisher **Normal / Rizzoli**
Category **Single Issue**
Date **Summer 1987**

Publication **San Francisco Focus**
Art Director **Matthew Drace**
Designer **Matthew Drace**
Photographer **Patricia Brabant**
Publisher **KQED**
Category **Single Issue**
Date **November 1, 1987**

114

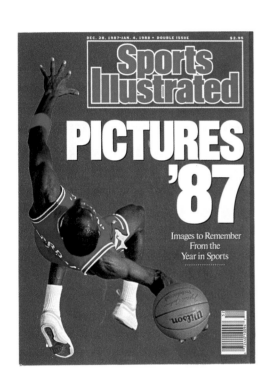

### Up to Their Same Old Tricks

I N May, former champions returned. The Edmonton Oilers, deposed a year earlier, held off the Philadelphia Flyers in seven games to win their third Stanley Cup in four years. Forty-seven-year-old Al Unser Sr., who hadn't won at Indianapolis since 1978, got a job as a fill-in driver and raced off with the fourth 500 victory of his career, tying a record set by A.J. Foyt. Meanwhile, the Brewers crashed to earth, losing 12 games in a row, and a colt named Alysheba, ridden by Chris McCarron, triumphed in both the Kentucky Derby and the Preakness to get two legs up on the Triple Crown.

*Pancho Carter flipped his car in Indy practice but suffered only a scratched helmet.*

*This backstroker's work done at the European championships in Strasbourg, France.*

*Dashing through the snow, these horses had a ball in St. Moritz's winter wonderland.*

Publication **Sports Illustrated**
Art Director **Steven Hoffman**
Designer **Peter Herbert**
Publisher **Time, Inc.**
Category **Single Issue**
Date **December 28 - January 4, 1987**

Publication **Warner Communications Annual Report**
Art Director **Peter Harrison**
Designer **Susan Hochbaum**
Photographer **Scott Morgan**
Client **Warner Communications, Inc.**
Agency **Pentagram Design**
Category **Single Issue**
Date **March 1987**

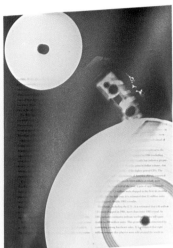

116

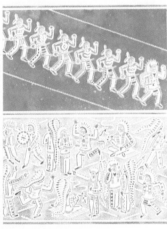

Publication **Drexel Burnham Lambert Annual Report**
Art Director **Colin Forbes**
Designer **Michael Gericke**
Illustrators **P. Leith, I. Von Treskow, Su Huntley, D. Muir,**
**S. Sterne, Ian Beck, G. Hardie, W. Schumaker, J. Field, P. Allen**
Photographer **Neil Selkirk**
Client **Drexel Burnham Lambert**
Agency **Pentagram Design**
Category **Single Issue**
Date **April 1987**

Publication **The New York Times Magazine / The New Season**
Art Director **David Barnett**
Designer **David Barnett**
Photographer **James Wojick**
Photo Editor **Haddas Dembo**
Publisher **The New York Times**
Category **Single Issue**
Date **August 30, 1987**

Publication **Life**
Art Director **Robin Brown**
Designer **Robin Brown**
Publisher **Time, Inc.**
Category **Single Issue**
Date **Fall 1987**

**118**

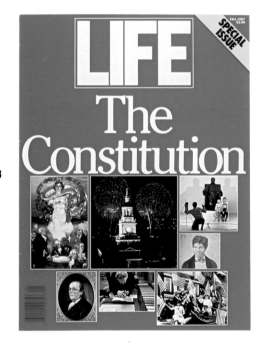

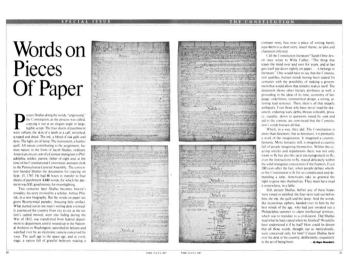

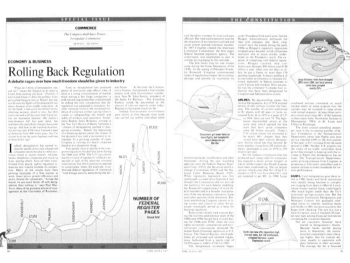

Publication **Time**
Art Director **Rudy Hoglund**
Designer **Tom Bentkowski**
Illustrator **Richard Hess**
Photographer **Various**
Publisher **Time, Inc.**
Category **Single Issue**
Date **July 6, 1987**

Publication **Boston Globe**
Art Director **Lynn Staley**
Designers **Lynn Staley, Holly Nixholm**
Publisher **Boston Globe**
Category **Single Issue**
Date **September 13, 1987**

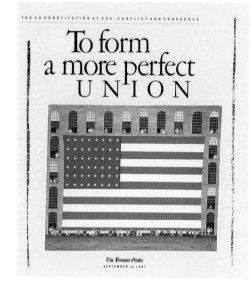

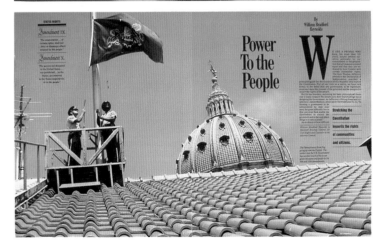

121

Publication **The New York Times Magazine**
Art Director **Diana LaGuardia**
Designers **Richard Semperi, Audrone Razgaitis,**
**Janet Froelich, Kevin McPhee**
Publisher **The New York Times**
Category **Single Issue**
Date **September 13, 1987**

Publication **Architectural Record**
Art Director **Alberto Bucchianeri**
Designers **Anna Egger-Schlesinger, Alberto Bucchianeri**
Publisher **McGraw-Hill, Inc.**
Category **Single Issue**
Date **Mid-September 1987**

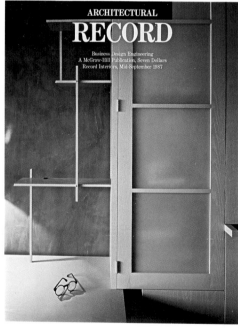

ARCHITECTURAL
# RECORD
Business Design Engineering
A McGraw-Hill Publication, Seven Dollars
Record Interiors, Mid-September 1987

## The world according to Starck

Portfolio
Philippe Starck, Designer

## Eye of his times

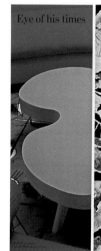

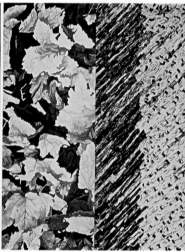

## Clothes make the man

*Three years ago Doug Tompkins decided to convert Esprit, the San Francisco-based clothing company he co-owns with wife Susie, from a wholesale to a retail operation. To do so, he enlisted the assistance of some of the architectural world's most creative talents.*

# The Villa Transformer

Schwartz/Pokovsky House
West Stockbridge, Massachusetts
Schwartz/Silver Architects

On Friday afternoons, Sheila Pokovsky and Warren Schwartz strap ten-month-old Julia Meryl into her car seat and head off to the family Honda for their place in the Berkshires. Judging by the cozy picture of domestic bliss that soon, dad, and the baby create, and by the modest builder's Colonial they occupy while there, one might envision their weekend retreat to be some sleepy clapboard cottage with leaky pipes, gingham curtains, and a sagging front porch. Not so. As the briefest glimpse confirms, the house at the end of the 600-yard drive from Newton to West Stockbridge is as alien to such preconceived notions of country life as any house could be imagined. In aloft-in fact, that some area residents think it looks like a UFO that has inexplicably, but permanently, touched down here in the land of Norman Rockwell. Others, naturally, see in the thirty-seven of aluminum star spools an obvious, if quirky, homage to Lady Liberty. And then there are those who are convinced that the owners took the old saw about a man's home being his "castle" a little too literally.

To explain the mystery of the quest title house on the hill, we must backtrack three years to the owners' honeymoon in Italy. (Where else could they go? He is an architect with Schwartz/Silver; she, a violinist with the Boston Symphony.) After the requisite nights in Venice, the newlyweds took the well-worn road west to pay their respects, predictably enough, to the 16th-century architecture of Vicenza and environs. Though duly impressed with the genius of Andrea Palladio's Villa Rotonda, it was Vincenzo Scamozzi's Villa Pisani at Lonigo that captured the honeymooners' hearts. When Schwartz and Pokovsky returned home, they carried with them a treasured souvenir: the image of the Villa Pisani's great octagon rising above its massive square base in a greasy knoll. It was then that Pokovsky decided she had had enough of blue-trim summer rentals during the Symphony's annual stint at Tanglewood, not surprisingly, when she suggested a new house to her new husband, the architect jumped at the design opportunity. The search for property that matched, more or less, the couple's memory of the Villa Pisani's site ended on a 16-acre hillside plot, six miles down the road from Tanglewood.

If Schwartz had cleverly conjed Scamozzi—doing the best he could with the $150,000 budget—we would have simply averted our eyes from the newly kitsch result, and plied the poor architect the derisions of grandeur. But Schwartz prefers to learn patiently, from one's inspiration, not facades, from tutory. True, the Villa Schwartz/Pokovsky owes much to the Villa Pisani, but the model has been so thoroughly reworked, so completely redrawn in Schwartz's own, idiosyncratic hand, that we regard the house as an original. Assuring, of course, are the sprightly details and peculiar apportionment that the architect devised to make Scamozzi's house his and Pokovsky's own: the massive, aluminum "eyebrows" around the windows and doors; the whimsical, perforated-metal pyramid that sits on the stair tower skylight, marking the outdoor from the indoor space—and, of course, the proud, jagged crown that ceremoniously solves that most basic of architectural problems—getting water off the roof. Schwartz's goal in these quirky announcements was to create a "timeless" building that would speak not only of the past but also of the future. For esthetics clues as to what the future looks like, he turned to those murderous-looking, Japanese toy soldiers of tomorrow ("transformers" in the ingressions), which arrive in 180 impossible decrepit pieces that only a child and Schwartz's whose collection recently topped the 400 mark) can figure out. One is relieved to note that, like the Scamozzi connection, the "Protean The War Lord" connection is more spiritual than literal.

Though Schwartz labels down his family getaway with a heavy referential package, the house shows no sign of strain. On the contrary, it exudes self-confidence. The key, of course, is control; knowing precisely—as Schwartz does—the point at which charming becomes cloying, serious becomes ponderous, clever becomes silly, proud becomes pompous, and playful becomes frivolous. *Charles K. Gandee*

Roger Herman House
Los Angeles
Frederick Fisher, Architect

## Collage with a view

This is the kind of house that seems possible only in Los Angeles. Floating above an expanse of modest bungalows, it looks hastily constructed, not quite permanently placed, like a great plywood ark unexpectedly washed up on the shore of Elysian Park. Its present form appears to be predicated on the simple idea of building as much space as possible for the least amount of money, to provide the client with a do-it-yourself shell with some hard sell over for a garden and the dogs. Whether or not it pleases the neighbors, who are still wondering when that house on the hill will ever be finished, is obviously irrelevant. This part of L. A. is, after all, a no-man's land sandwiched between Dodger Stadium and the Golden State Freeway, a frontier of sorts even for the locals.

But don't let the rough exterior fool you—the Herman house is a very much designed. If the cheap materials, ad-hoc composition, and offhand detailing employed by its architect, Frederick Fisher, seem unorthodox to some, others will instantly identify them as the current parlance of Southern California architecture. The master of this idiom, of course, is Frank O. Gehry, with whom Fisher once apprenticed. Like his former employer, Fisher is fond of the wrenched and the raw, and aligns himself with artists—both as collaborators and clients—to achieve the unexpected an approach that resulted, for example, in a joint project with artist Eric Orr to transform the upper floors of a former factory, into an external loft with waterfall for a painter and her husband. (RECORD, February 1985, pages 136-141).

For his latest project, Fisher was fortunate enough to be commissioned by Roger Herman, an energetic German-born painter whose expressionistic canvases often depict shadowy buildings. That architect and artist should combine their talents in the design of the house was immediately understood. Their collaboration began with organizing a layout of multifunctional rooms modeled on Herman's former warehouse loft, a ground-floor painting studio, a second-story space comprising the kitchen, living, and dining "rooms," and a pair of bedrooms that also serve as study/workrooms, linked by a series of decks. A third bedroom, originally developed as a freestanding box on the roof, was extended from the mass of the house to satisfy the artist's preference for the image of a turreted castle. Pleased with the solution, Herman was inspired enough to paint a portrait of the house soon after the first model was completed (left).

Fisher, who humbly characterizes his role in the design of the house as "keeping the facades coherent and creating a way to naturally light the interiors," likens the collaborative process to creating a collage. His method of assemblage is distinguished from that of the L. A. contemporaries by a preference for the graphic over the sculptural, a reconstruction of overlapping planes rather than of disjointed volumes. The elevations of the Herman house, for example, recompense stack-framed windows re-arranged by the client from an industrial building demolished near his previous studio, as well as sunlit custom components as the 16-foot-high front door, proportioned to accommodate large canvases. Punctuated by the roof deck that projects between the living area and bedroom "towers," the rectilinear pattern of openings and pivoted panels on the street facade creates a self-contained monumentality that belies the wedge shape of the house and the sequence of distinct rooms contained within. Fisher's skill is composing mundane architectural elements into planar abstractions of seasoned geometries extends to the interiors, where natural illumination is manipulated through skylights and windows to bathe walls and ceilings with sheets of light. Though the architect claims that the rational for the design is based on economy—"a tight budget forces you to make decisions that don't depend on the details"—its no-frills, no-gimmicks esthetic has exerted a profound effect on Herman. The artist has not only begun to paint more images of simple, boxy architecture, but has designed a building: a plywood doghouse for his two Great Danes. *D. K. D.*

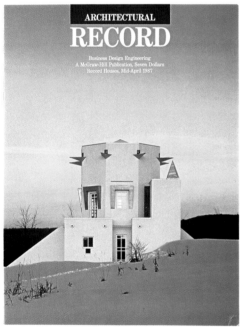

123

Publication **Architectural Record**
Art Director **Alberto Bucchianeri**
Designers **Anna Egger-Schlesinger, Alberto Bucchianeri**
Photographer **Tim Street-Porter**
Publisher **McGraw-Hill, Inc.**
Category **Single Issue**
Date **Mid-April 1987**

Publication **New England Monthly**
Art Directors **Hans Teensma, Mark Danzig**
Designer **Hans Teensma**
Photographer **George Lange**
Photo Editor **John Faymon**
Publisher **New England Monthly, Inc.**
Category **Special Section**
Date **July 1987**

MENU

*Big Glen's*
*All New England*
*Super Diner*

# The Man Who Ate New England

BY GLEN WAGGONER

### Gateway to Heaven

### Pound for Pound

### Stand Up and Be Counted

### Basic Diner Tactics 101

### Stuffy?

### Dog Race

### Hall of Fame

### May I Take Your Order?

### Clam Chowder: A Minority View

### Check, Please

NEW ENGLAND MONTHLY

NEW ENGLAND MONTHLY

LOCAL HEROES

*Some you know, most you've never heard of. Together, they comprise a portrait of our region at its very best. Without them, and without thousands more like them, we would be something very different: we wouldn't be New England.*

THE TRIALS
OF DEN VO

*By* JOHN TAYMAN
*Photography by* JERRY BERNDT

He has become the Boston Police Department's best weapon in its war with the Vietnamese street gangs.

Her life still has its share of two-hundred-dollar gigs — given her talent, more than its share.

125

The Art of the Canoe

Silent Music

Publication **New England Monthly**
Art Directors **Hans Teensma, Mark Danzig**
Designers **Hans Teensma, Mark Danzig**
Photo Editor **John Tayman**
Publisher **New England Monthly, Inc.**
Category **Special Section**
Date **September 1987**

Publication **Spy**
Art Director **Alexander Isley**
Designers **Alexander Isley, Sonda Andersson,**
**Catherine Gilmore-Barnes**
Photo Editor **Amy Stark**
Publisher **Spy Publishing Partners**
Category **Single Issue**
Date **September 1987**

For many people, life is a series of high-stakes business deals, ferociously pursued—including courtship and marriage. Yes, this is 1987; loveless marriage is chic again. And even though we, like you, find the whole business appalling and sad and sordid and vulgar, once we started, we couldn't stop listening to NELL SCOVELL explain

*How to Marry a*

M

illionaire

Gayfryd Steinberg grew up in a rented house in Vancouver, British Columbia, the daughter of a telephone company clerk. Today she lives with her husband, the overfed conglomerateur Saul Steinberg, in an art-clogged Park Avenue triplex that used to belong to John D. Rockefeller Jr. The apartment measures roughly 28,000 square feet, larger than Tiffany's three sales floors combined. Paintings by Titian, Rubens and Frans Hals hang in the public rooms. A lesser artist such as Renoir is placed in Gayfryd Steinberg's powder room.

Barbara "Basia" Piasecka Johnson emigrated from Poland in 1968 with

$100 and sufficient cleaning skills to get a chambermaid's job in the home of J. Seward Johnson, the late nutty Johnson & Johnson heir and marine biology buff. Three years later she had stopped doing windows, married her boss and begun overseeing construction of Jasna Polana ("Bright Meadow"), a $30 million Palladian mansion of wretched excess on 140 acres in Princeton, New Jersey. The grounds include a 72-foot-long swimming pool surrounded by Greek and Roman antiquities

GOLD-
diggers
of 1987

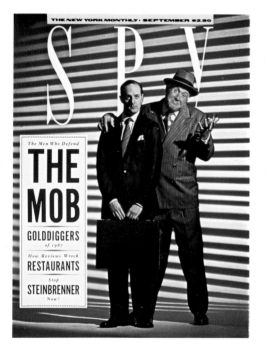

NEVER MIND the felony conviction and the braggadocio and the double knits and the triple chin—the Yankees' loathsome, loudmouthed owner qualifies as a blot on the landscape for professional-reasons alone. ED KIERSH proves, once and for all, that the players Steinbrenner trades for are invariably losers—while the ones he trades away are soon performing like Hall of Famers.

*Damn*Yankee

How
*George Steinbrenner*
BEFOULED
NEW YORK
BASEBALL

"LET'S NOT DO IT, GEORGE—IT'S A BAD DEAL," the Yankee brain trust cried. "Wait a while—maybe we'll pick up a better player later."

As more dreaming shouts filled the Hollywood, Florida, hotel room, a few men sipped coffee or anxiously flipped through their bible, *The Baseball Encyclopedia.* This group, tan and dressed for the golf course, normally enjoyed wheeling and dealing in ballplayers; they had gathered there last December for that express purpose. But this particular trade—giving away the Yankees' Mike Easler to get the Phillies' Charles Hudson—was different. It was being forced upon them.

Against the advice of counselors specifically hired to ferret out talent, George Steinbrenner, the Yankees' principal owner, gave up Easler, a dependable .302 hitter, for Hudson, a right-handed pitcher with a lifetime record of 32 wins and 42 losses.

It proved to be another Steinbrenner quick hit, another strange bloodletting. Hudson, after winning his first six games for the

You've heard it,
we've heard it—our
American system
of justice requires that
every defendant,
no matter how vicious
or contemptible,
receive the best
legal defense
possible. But do
gangster apologists

The men who defend

THE
MOB

really believe
they're performing
a public service?
Do Mafia mouthpieces
really believe the
Mafia doesn't exist?
Who's kidding
whom? JAMES TRAUB
cross-examined
six high-powered
members of the
black-collar bar and
came back with
an unprecedented
group portrait

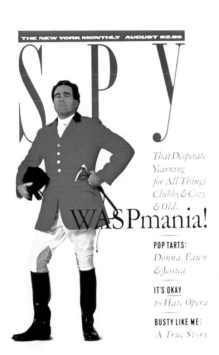

THE NEW YORK MONTHLY · AUGUST $2.50

# SPY

*That Desperate
Yearning
for All Things
Clubby & Cozy
& Old:*

## WASPmania!

**POP TARTS:**
*Donna, Faun
& Jessica*

**IT'S OKAY**
*to Hate Opera*

**BUSTY LIKE ME:**
*A True Story*

THE SPY INTERVIEW

# Big,
Rich
& Pushy:
Jake

**HEY, GANG!** Let's join leading fitness author, top character actor, home-video star—*don't quit!*—successful businessman, public activist for national—*don't quit!*—fitness, motivational expert, "international energizer," ubiquitous spokesperson (and colorful and caring personality in his own right) Jake "Body by Jake" Steinfeld for an interview that is close up and personal. Jake's former schoolmate, journalist SUSAN CHUMSKY, leads the workout. *Let's go!* And remember: *you're all a bunch of winners!*

*How fabulous our noble chintz,
Our whatnots filled with treen;
Our antique studs and sporting prints,
Our knocked-off L. L. Bean!*

# WASPmania!

THEY'VE MADE THEIR BUCKETS OF MONEY AND NOW THEY WANT TO LIVE LIKE THE OLD-MONEYED CLASSES. THEY'RE CORNERING THE WORLD'S SUPPLY OF CHINTZ AND SILVER PICTURE FRAMES AND GEORGE STUBBS PAINTINGS AND PETIT POINT-COVERED OTTOMANS. THEY'RE READING UP ON DECENT PORT VINTAGES AND SENDING THEIR OVERFED CHILDREN TO MANNERS CLASSES. BEFORE OUR VERY EYES, ORDINARY MEN AND WOMEN—REALLY ORDINARY MEN AND WOMEN—ARE TURNING THEMSELVES INTO MAKE BELIEVE WHITE ANGLO-SAXON PROTESTANTS. MICHAEL THOMAS HIKES UP HIS SUSPENDERS—ER, BRACES—TO EXAMINE THE SORRY SIGHT OF A NEW YORK CAUGHT IN THE GILT-EDGED GRIP OF RAMPANT WASPMANIA.

*So come to us, you newly rich,
No longer ranked as dreck;
Here instant class
Is brought to pass—
We need nothing but your check!*

# It's Okay

## to

IT'S OKAY TO HATE POETRY

There are three titanic hoaxes, a cultural triad no human has ever enjoyed for even a millisecond:

IT'S OKAY TO HATE OPERA

## Hate

poetry, opera and ballet. Each claims a massive,

IT'S OKAY TO HATE BALLET

## High

often hysteric following, each rakes in substantial

## Culture

moneys, each has an obscenely enduring history.

A RUDE MANIFESTO
BY PAUL RUDNICK

AND EACH REMAINS A WHOLE AND UTTER FRAUD, A DIABOLIC PUNISHMENT, AN ALL-DEVOURING LIE. THESE ITEMS ARE, IF NOT DISTINCTIVELY EVIL, AT BEST CON JOBS ON A GALACTIC SCALE.

**POETRY:** SMALL AND FEY. Poetry is simply poor punctuation. A poem is a thought unworthy of a paragraph, random words tossed on the page, literary lint. Poems are Laura Ashley prints for the mind, unicorn dung. They possess none of the time-honored virtues of fine literature: you can't curl up with a nice trashy poem. Poems are rarely adapted as miniseries. Your parents would never forbid you to bring that Jackie Collins poem into the house; a volume of Millay seldom falls open to the good parts. People never bicker over who should play Tiresias in "The Waste Land," Valerie Bertinelli or Pam Dawber. Why are poems composed, or perpetrated? To break up the page in *The New Yorker*. Without poetry Ann Beattie would smash into the cartoons, and the right parts on ice making would hurtle against the windbreaker ads. Without poetry high school girls in corduroy jumpers and black leotards might have to make some friends. Emily Dickinson never left her cottage in Amherst, and with just cause: no one asked her to. *Don't invite Emily, she might recite one of her things.* Scholars swear that Shakespeare didn't exist, that his verse was penned by Ben Jonson or Marlowe (under a pseudonym, so they wouldn't be blamed). Has anyone ever got lucky after pulling, "Hey, babe, read any good poems lately?"
As with all operas and ballets, all poems are identical. If you must, skim two lines of any poem, shudder and know the truth. That's right, they all mention "love's fragrant bower." And silvery snowflakes and autumn's pungent grief and echoing silence and little cat feet. You never have to read another, like the actors in *Platoon*, you have tasted hell and survived.

**OPERA:** BIG AND EMBARRASSING. Opera is even more loathsome than poetry, with opera, you've paid a lot of money and you're physically trapped. You're stuck sitting there while

AUGUST 1987 SPY 61

Publication **Spy**
Art Director **Alexander Isley**
Designers **Alexander Isley, Sonda Andersson,**
**Catherine Gilmore-Barnes**
Photo Editor **Amy Stark**
Publisher **Spy Publishing Partners**
Category **Single Issue**
Date **August 1987**

Publication **Spy**
Art Director **Alexander Isley**
Designers **Alexander Knowlton, Alexander Isley,**
**Catherine Gilmore-Barnes**
Publisher **Spy Publishing Partners**
Category **Single Issue**
Date **December 1987**

128

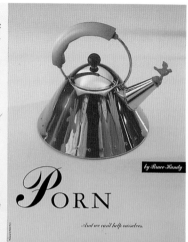

### IT'S YUPPIE PORN

*by Bruce Handy*

*And we can't help ourselves.*

### Separated at Birth?

*The Unabridged Edition*

### doing business *broke*

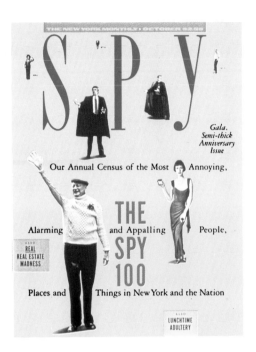

Publication **Spy**
Art Director **Alexander Isley**
Designers **Alexander Isley, Catherine Gilmore-Barnes**
Photo Editor **Amy Stark**
Publisher **Spy Publishing Partners**
Category **Single Issue**
Date **October 1987**

Publication **Isabella Stewart Gardner Museum/**
**Fund-Raising Brochure**
Art Director **Jack Wolff**
Designer **Jack Wolff**
Client **Isabella Stewart Gardner Museum**
Agency **Jan Krukowsi Associates**
Category **Single Issue**
Date **December 1987**

130

## *Portrait of the Museum*

This remarkable institution is the achievement of one person. Isabella Stewart Gardner (1840–1924) fulfilled all the functions necessary to a museum: she selected the objects, paid for them, designed the building, installed the collection, and presided as director. By the terms of her will nothing may be added to the galleries and the arrangement remains as she left it. She also believed that works of art should be displayed in a setting that would fire the imagination. Every gallery has a character of its own, and works of art are arranged without regard to chronology or origin. Music and flowers are the natural accompaniment to the visual arts, Mrs. Gardner believed, and a place was provided for them. The building, her interpretation of a fifteenth-century Venetian palazzo, adds to the illusion of being in a private house on which each generation has left its mark.

"If you have time to do only one thing, go to the Gardner Museum," is often the advice given to world travelers who arrive in Boston for the first time. Built with a concept of eternity, yet rooted in the *fin-de-siècle*, it has the founder's forceful sense of what a museum should be. First, there are great paintings. To balance the paintings, rooms are filled with sculpture and furniture, and textiles are everywhere – hung on the walls, placed on tables – often under an array of smaller objects. With each change of season the quality of light changes, and may be best after a new fallen snow.

Visitors linger in the Court, or pause in the balconies above, looking down on the flowering plants or across the way to glimpse a particularly fine piece framed by a window. People return time and again to see familiar favorites, and yet leave with a sense of surprise at having discovered something new.

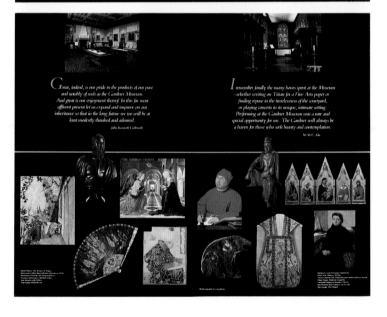

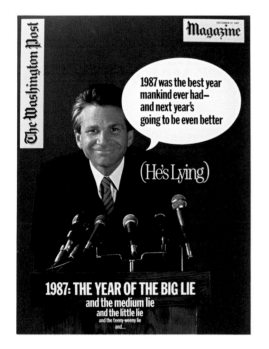

Publication **The Washington Post Magazine**
Art Director **Brian Noyes**
Designer **Brian Noyes**
Illustrators **Anita Kunz, James Ynag, Steve Brodner**
Photo Editor **Molly Roberts**
Publisher **The Washington Post**
Category **Single Issue**
Date **December 27, 1987**

Publication **The Quality Review**
Art Director **Peter Deutsch**
Designer **Peter Deutsch**
Illustrators **Jean-Christian Knaff, Regan Dunnick, Pierre Le-Tan**
Photographers **Gloria Baker, Neal Slavin, Steve Hill**
Client **American Society for Quality Control**
Agency **Deutsch Design, Inc.**
Category **Single Issue**
Date **Fall 1987**

132

Plate 3.

# Maya Angelou Says

Musings on quality
by a woman whose lifework
represents excellence.

Publication **Royal Viking "Skald"**
Art Director **Kit Hinrichs**
Designers **Kit Hinrichs, Karen Berndt**
Illustrators **Dave Stevenson, Mark Summers, Michael Bull**
Photographers **Michele Clement, Terry Heffernan,**
**Barry Robinson, Harvey Lloyd**
Client **Royal Viking Lines**
Agency **Pentagram Design**
Category **Single Issue**
Date **Fall 1987**

Publication **Mercedes**
Art Director **John Tom Cohoe**
Designer **John Tom Cohoe**
Photographers **Clint Clemens, Bob Grigg, Jeff Zwart,**
**Brad Miller**
Client **Mercedes-Benz of North America**
Agency **McCaffrey & McCall**
Category **Single Issue**
Date **September 1987**

Now and then, Mercedes-Benz moves from one model year to the next with scarcely a break in stride—well, in all, only polite acknowledgment that this threshold has arrived. Such behavior from Mercedes-Benz should not be surprising. No other car company has witnessed the onset of as many model years. (One hundred and

two, to be exact.)
It therefore comes as a distinct pleasure to announce the notable and exciting Mercedes-Benz revisions for 1988.
The S-Class expands with the 300SEL—the first long-wheelbase sedan with a gasoline six-cylinder Mercedes-Benz has offered in America since 1971. Also, the enhanced stereo radio

and cassette player fitted across the line for 1988 becomes, in every S-Class sedan and coupe, a 100-watt, ten-speaker sound system.
The 300 Class gains, of course, the new 300CE Coupe (shown at its C-pillar). Other significant 300 Class news, and another company first in America, a gasoline-powered station wagon, the six-cylinder 300TE, is now

available.
The 190 Class for 1988 returns with a choice of three trim, agile automobiles: the 190E 2.3, the 190E 2.6 Sedans, and 190D 2.5.
The following pages contain brief descriptions of each 1988 model. Detailed information will be gladly provided by an authorized Mercedes-Benz dealer.

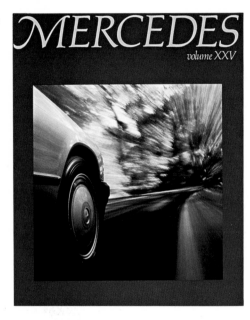

the vertical and dip to the rear deck lid, which is 1.4 inches lower than on the sedan, in a smooth, sensuous sweep. The rear window panel smoothly overlaps into the roof and C-pillars, forming an integrated, harmonious line. Streamlined protective lower body panels extend from the coupe's front wheels to the rear. The new coupe's system of air management tells us not only its remarkably low 0.30 coefficient of aerodynamic drag, but also in the quiet of the cabin, at high speed, with even one window down.

## 300 CE

Elegance. Movement. Sensuality. Power. Classic coupes hold a breathless excitement in their essence. The 1988 300CE, pictured here and on the following pages, is a coupe for the 300 Class with a truly breathtaking shape.
The 300CE Coupe bears a close family resemblance to the Mercedes-Benz 300 Class sedans—from its aerodynamically angled grille to its superb, powerful, smooth-running, 177-hp, in-line six-cylinder engine. But its new body, 5.3 inches shorter in wheelbase

and 1.4 inches lower than the sedan, marks it exclusively as a powerful grand touring car. The more compact dimensions of a coupe challenged Mercedes-Benz engineers to carefully alter the 300 Class body design and reinforce the chassis—a challenge from which elegant solutions emerged. B-pillars have been cleverly eliminated, making the rolled up windows appear to be one solid panel that virtually blends into the exterior skin. The C-pillars are gently raked at 25 degrees from

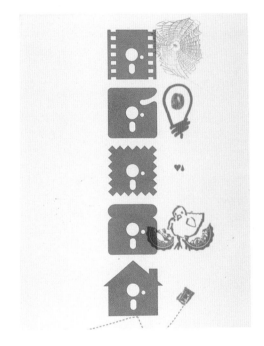

Publication **Prattonia**
Art Directors **Samuel Kuo, Megan Cash**
Designers **Samuel Kuo, Megan Cash, Tony Mennuto, Ryan Ng**
Illustrator **Various**
Photographer **Various**
Publisher **Pratt Institute**
Category **Single Issue**
Date **January 1987**

Publication **Spirit News**
Art Director **Ron Sullivan**
Designers **J. Flaming, W. Baronet, L. Helton, D. McKnight,**
**D. Kolosta, M. Spring, A. Garcia**
Illustrators **Darrel Kolosta, Jon Flaming, Linda Helton,**
**Art Garcia**
Photographers **Michael Johnson, Tom Ryan**
Client **Cheerleader Supply Company**
Agency **Sullivan Perkins**
Category **Single Issue**
Date **October 1, 1987**

136

Publication **Seventy-Six**

Art Director **Ray Engle**

Designer **Debra Hampton**

Illustrator **Debra Hampton**

Photographer **Joe Maddocks**

Photo Editor **Tim Smight**

Client **Unocal Corporation**

Agency **Ray Engle & Associates**

Category **Single Issue**

Date **Fall 1987**

137

Publication **Shercorp Annual Report**
Art Director **Dennis P. Moran**
Designer **Ralph James Russini**
Photographer **Lynn Johnson**
Photo Editor **Ralph James Russini**
Client **Shercorp / Shadyside Hospital**
Agency **Adam, Filippo & Moran, Inc.**
Category **Single Issue**
Date **May 15, 1987**

Publication **Pacific Financial Annual Report**
Art Director **Ken White**
Designer **Lisa Levin**
Photographer **Eric Myer**
Client **Pacific Financial Companies**
Agency **Ken White & Associates**
Category **Single Issue**
Date **April 1987**

Publication **Intertrans Annual Report**
Art Director **Ron Sullivan**
Designer **Willie Baronet**
Illustrator **Willie Baronet**
Photographer **Gerry Kano**
Client **Intertrans, Inc.**
Agency **Sullivan Perkins**
Category **Single Issue**
Date **December 31, 1987**

INTERTRANS CORPORATION ANNUAL REPORT 1986

140

Publication **H.J. Heinz Company Annual Report**
Art Director **Bennett Robinson**
Designers **Bennett Robinson, Erika Siegel**
Photographer **Rodney Smith**
Client **H.J. Heinz Company**
Agency **Corporate Graphics, Inc.**
Category **Single Issue**
Date **July 1987**

Publication **Immunex Annual Report**
Art Director **Kit Hinrichs**
Designers **Kit Hinrichs, Belle How**
Illustrator **Vincent Perez**
Photographer **Steve Firebaugh**
Client **Immunex Corporation**
Agency **Pentagram Design**
Category **Single Issue**
Date **March 1, 1987**

142

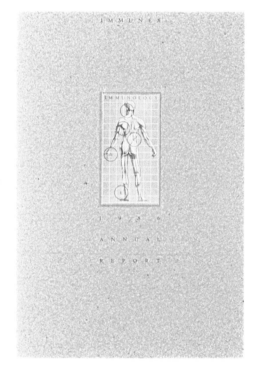

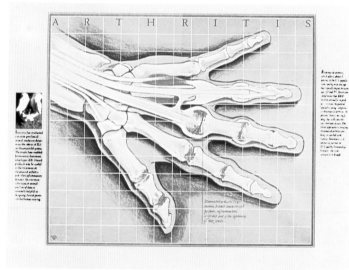

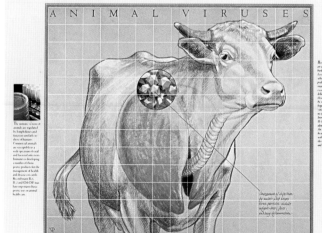

1 9 8 7 Annual Report

A Season of Growth

Goucher College

FINANCIAL REVIEW

*The foresight and generosity of Goucher's alumni and friends have contributed tremendously to the successful growth of the college.*

*"Not a having and a resting, but a growing and a becoming, is the character of perfection as culture conceives it."*
Matthew Arnold, Sweetness and Light

Strawberry – foresight, good works

THE FLOWERING OF GOUCHER

*"If you can look into the seeds of time, And say which grain will grow and which will not, Speak."*
William Shakespeare, Macbeth

Violet – devotion, faithfulness

**Alumni recruitment blossoms**
Nancy-Betts Hay '63 remembers the telephone call from Goucher President Rhoda Dorsey in November 1976. The college was launching a new program to boost enrollment. The then-novel idea was to use alumni as admissions recruiters. Would Ms. Hay be interested in applying for the job? As it happened, three talented alumnae who were looking for part-time work – Ms. Hay, Sally Austin '57 and Janet Kantor '55 – decided to offer their pooled services to Goucher. The AAR (Alumni Admissions Recruitment) Program was born. The three soon discovered that they had tapped a rich vein of alumni enthusiasm. "Helping with recruitment was a perfect outlet for alumni who wanted to get involved with the college but were limited by time and location," Ms. Hay notes.

Carol Krugman '70 was one of the first alumni volunteers. She was living in Denver and had little time but a great deal of desire to help. "I felt that I had gotten so much from the school that I could spend a lifetime trying to repay Goucher... this was something I could do." Ms. Krugman carried her commitment through moves to South Carolina and New York City, where she is now vice president/projects director for World Health Communications Inc. and regional AAR captain for New York City. She has seen many changes in the program since those early days. But the greatest changes of all, she says, have been in the past two years. The numbers tell part of the story. From 50 volunteers in the program's first year to 330, located in 48 states and one foreign country today; from an initial policy of no alumni interviews with prospective students to almost 200 interviews by alumni recruiters last year, the AAR program has grown, prospered – and diversified. "In the past few years we've achieved a greater degree of respect both within the college and in our communities," notes Mary Ann Zavulakis Jackson '56, California regional captain and veteran of the program. "Here in California, continuity has been tremendously important. The high school counselors now know that we're here to stay; they can depend on us." Also central to the program's success, says Ms. Jackson, was Goucher's decision two years ago to hire a full-time professional, Vicki Cohen '79, as coordinator of volunteer programs. "We may be located all over the country, but we know we have a focal point, a person to call for whatever we need," and indeed, as the competition among colleges for students has become fiercer, Ms. Cohen notes that recognition of the value of alumni recruiters has grown. "The AARs play a vital role in helping to find students all over the country who can benefit the most from a Goucher education. Their work with individual students is so extensive; they make each applicant feel as if he or she has an advocate in the Admissions Office." A thorough knowledge of the college – obtained through annual training and information sessions at Alumni Council, a quarterly newsletters, and numerous phone calls and visits by Admissions office staff members with AARs – contributes to each AAR's effectiveness as a spokesperson at high schools and

Publication **1987 Goucher College Annual Report**
Art Directors **Anthony Rutka, Kate Bergquist**
Designer **Kate Bergquist**
Illustrator **Kate Bergquist**
Photographer **Bill Denison**
Client **Goucher College**
Agency **Rutka / Weadcock Design**
Category **Single Issue**
Date **November 30, 1987**

Publication **New York**
Art Director **Robert Best**
Designers **Josh Gosfield, Betsy Welsh, Deborah Quintana**
Photo Editor **Jordan Schaps**
Agency **News Group America**
Category **Special Section**
Date **June 29 - July 6, 1987**

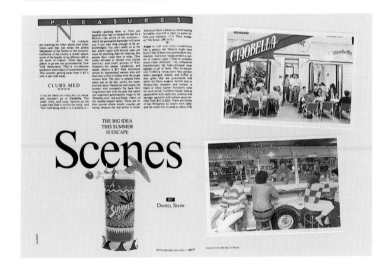

144

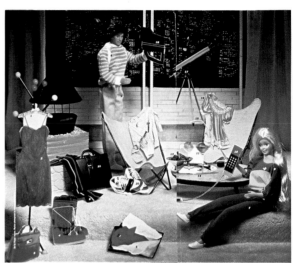

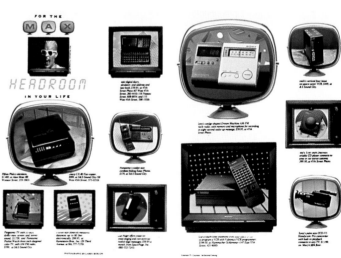

Publication **New York**
Art Director **Robert Best**
Designers **Josh Gosfield, Betsy Welsh, Deborah Quintana**
Illustrator **Dan Kirk**
Publisher **News Group America**
Category **Special Section**
Date **December 7, 1987**

Publication **New York**
Art Director **Robert Best**
Designers **Josh Gosfield, Betsy Welsh, Deborah Quintana**
Publisher **News Group America**
Category **Special Section and Single Issue**
Date **November 23, 1987**

### MIGUEL BAEZ
# Heartthrob Toreador

MIGUEL BAEZ, HERO OF THE SPANISH BULLRING, SAYS HIS BIGGEST KICK IN LIFE IS CUTTING EARS. THE SON OF LITRI, THE GREAT SPANISH BULLFIGHTER OF THE '60s, BAEZ COMES BY HIS PASSION NATURALLY. THE AWARD FOR SUPERIOR PERFORMANCE IN THE RING BEING THE EARS OF THE vanquished beast.

### PAULINA PORIZKOVA
# The Model of Perfection

I CAN BE QUITE A BUBBLEHEAD," SAYS $5,000-A-DAY MODEL PAULINA PORIZKOVA. "IF I GET BORED I DRESS UP, OR ELSE I DO MY JACK NICHOLSON IMPERSONATION." SHE DEMONSTRATES THIS BY PULLING HER HAIR BACK AND MIMICKING NICHOLSON'S ARCHING BROW and demonic smile.

### ANNIE PUJOL
# Vanna Goes Gallic

HEY, WAIT A MINUTE! DON'T TOUCH THAT DIAL—THERE'S THE SAME FABULOUS WHEEL, THE SAME GLITTERING BOARD, THE SAME SIMULATED LEATHERETTE LIVING ROOM SET. IN FACT, IT'S A LINE-FOR-LINE COPY OF AMERICA'S MOST BELOVED GAME SHOW, *WHEEL OF FORTUNE*, but everybody's, now dive, speaking French.

### MARIO TAMAYO
# L.A.'s Impresario of Hip

IF LOS ANGELES IN THE LATE '80s IS BEGINNING TO SEEM LIKE ONE LONG PARTY, COLOMBIAN-BORN MARIO TAMAYO, 29, HAS TO QUALIFY AS ONE OF THE PARTY'S HOTTEST HOSTS. HIS SUNNY, PASTEL-PAINTED CAFE MAMBO IS AROUND THE CORNER FROM HIS NEW art gallery, which is a few blocks away from Cha Cha Cha.

### SUE CHOI
# Professional Party Girl

SUE CHOI, NIGHTCLUB OWNER, SAYS, "I WAS NEVER REALLY ATTRACTED TO THE CLUB SCENE BEFORE THIS." THE KOREAN-BORN IMPRESARIO, ALONG WITH HER BOYFRIEND FREDERIC MESCHIN AND HIS BROTHER NICOLAS, OWNS FLAMING COLOSSUS—LOS ANGELES' HOTTEST CLUB-OF-THE-MOMENT.

VICTOIRE SCHLUMBERGER ③

FUN

### ZARA METCALFE
# D-Girl With Lots of Stories

ZARA METCALFE IS WHAT THE FILM INDUSTRY REFERS TO AS A D-GIRL. THE "D" STANDS FOR DEVELOPMENT, THE "GIRL" FOR THE LINGERING SEXISM THAT HAUNTS HOLLYWOOD. UNDAUNTED, METCALFE SEARCHES FOR PROPERTIES OR IDEAS THAT DIRECTORS CAN DEVELOP INTO MOVIES.

TAMA JANOWITZ ④

Publication **Scene**
Art Director **Edward Leida**
Designers **Edward Leida, Kirby Rodriguez**
Photographer **James Brill**
Publisher **Fairchild Publications**
Category **Special Section**
Date **December 1987**

Publication **Time**
Art Director **Rudy Hoglund**
Designer **Arthur Hochstein**
Photographer **Philip Mehta**
Photo Editor **Arnold Drapkin**
Publisher **Time, Inc.**
Category **Special Section**
Date **October 26, 1987**

**148**

# IMAGES 19 87

"This treaty represents a landmark in postwar history."
*Ronald Reagan*
*On the intermediate nuclear forces pact*

"We can be proud of planting this sapling . . . But it is probably still too early to bestow laurels upon each other."
*Mikhail Gorbachev*

*The New York Times*
REAGAN AND GORBACHEV SIGN MISSILE TREATY AND VOW TO WORK FOR GREATER REDUCTIONS

# IMAGES 19 87

"No institution can by itself replace . . . human love or human initiative, when it is a question of dealing with the suffering of another."
*Pope John Paul II*
*Pictured with a young AIDS victim*

OBSERVER
The day terror came to a peasant village

"They had died of suffocation. Their . . . bodies remained crouching, cuddled together, like the corpses at Pompeii."
*London Observer*
*On the bombing of an Afghan village by Soviet SU-17s that killed this mother and her children*

*San Francisco Examiner*
SOUVENIR EDITION
Pope embraces The City

# IMAGES

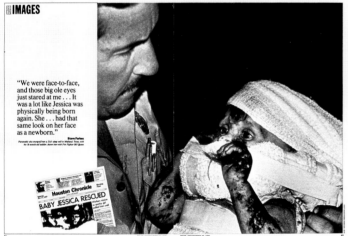

"We were face-to-face, and those big ole eyes just stared at me . . . It was a lot like Jessica was physically being born again. She . . . had that same look on her face as a newborn."
*Steve Forbes*
*Paramedic who emerged from a 22-ft.-deep well in Midland, Texas, with the 18-month-old toddler, shown here with Fire Fighter Bill Quan*

*Houston Chronicle*
BABY JESSICA RESCUED

# IMAGES

"There is nothing better for the inside of a man than the outside of a horse."
*Ronald Reagan*
*President*

"I haven't been spending much time on tractors of late."
*Albert Gore*
*Aspiring to be President*

"The rule used to be 'What am I saying?' Now it is 'How do I appear?'"
*Alexander Haig*
*Republican contender*

"We are reaching out, and people are responding."
*Jesse Jackson*
*Democratic contender*

*USA TODAY*
What we want in a president

Publication **Time**
Art Director **Rudy Hoglund**
Designer **E. Genevieve Williams**
Photographers **Pete Souza, Bill Pierce, John Gaps**
Publisher **Time, Inc.**
Category **Special Section**
Date **December 28, 1987**

Publication **Time**
Art Director **Rudy Hoglund**
Designer **Tom Bentkowski**
Publisher **Time, Inc.**
Category **Special Section**
Date **February 23, 1987**

ESSAY
# An African Journey

Photographs for Time
by Neil Leifer

W

E CARRY
WITH US THE WONDERS WE SEEK
WITHOUT US. THERE IS ALL
AFRICA AND HER PRODIGIES IN US.
—SIR THOMAS BROWNE

T

O SEE TEN
THOUSAND ANIMALS UNTAMED
AND NOT BRANDED WITH
THE SYMBOLS OF HUMAN
COMMERCE IS LIKE SCALING
AN UNCONQUERED MOUNTAIN
FOR THE FIRST TIME, OR LIKE
FINDING A FOREST WITHOUT
ROADS OR FOOTPATHS
OR THE BLEMISH OF AN AXE
—BERYL MARKHAM

T

HE LAND TEEMS
INFINITE IN NUMBER AND
INCREDIBLE IN VARIETY. IT HOLDS
THE FIERCEST BEASTS OF RAVIN, AND
THE FLEETEST AND MOST TIMID OF
THOSE BEINGS THAT LIVE IN
... THERE ARE CREATURES WHICH
ARE THE EMBODIMENTS OF GRACE,
AND OTHERS WHOSE HUGE
UNGAINLINESS IS LIKE THAT
OF A SHAPE IN A NIGHTMARE.
—THEODORE ROOSEVELT

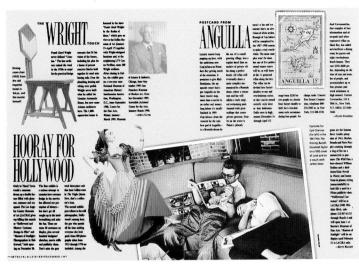

## THE WRIGHT TOUCH

## POSTCARD FROM ANGUILLA

## HOORAY FOR HOLLYWOOD

## POSTCARD FROM HONOLULU

## SMALL BYTES OF PARIS

## TREASURES FROM TUNISIA

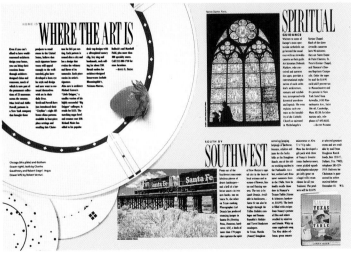

## WHERE THE ART IS

## SPIRITUAL GUIDANCE

## SOUTH BY SOUTHWEST

## GREAT GIFTS THAT TRAVEL WELL

## TAKING OFF

EDITED BY WILLIAM SERTL

Publication **Travel & Leisure**
Art Director **Bob Ciano**
Designer **Joe Paschke**
Photo Editor **Eileen M. Smith**
Publisher **American Express**
Category **Special Section**
Date **December 1987**

Publication **Premiere**
Art Directors **David Walters, Robert Best**
Designers **David Walters, Robert Best**
Publisher **Murdoch / Hachette**
Category **Special Section**
Date **Several 1987**

152

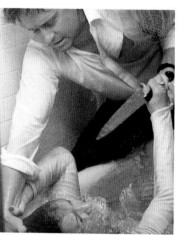

# PREMIERE

## THE PHONE

## PREMIERE

## HOLLYWOODESE

## PREMIERE

## PER DIEM

## PREMIERE

## THE WORD

Publication **Premiere**
Art Directors **David Walters, Robert Best**
Designers **Robert Best, David Walters**
Design Directors **Robert Best, Daniel Kirk**
Photographer **David Kelley**
Publisher **Murdoch / Hachette**
Category **Special Section**
Date **July / Aug, Oct, Nov, Dec, 1987**

Publication **San Francisco Focus**
Art Director **Matthew Drace**
Designer **Mark Ulriksen**
Illustrator **Tim Carroll**
Publisher **KQED**
Category **Special Section**
Date **August 1, 1987**

154

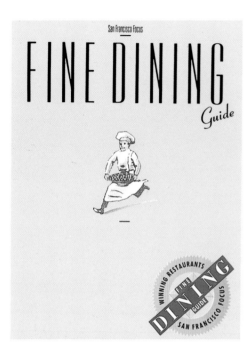

San Francisco Focus

# FINE DINING
*Guide*

WINNING RESTAURANTS
FINE DINING GUIDE
SAN FRANCISCO FOCUS

# LET'S *Eat*

Ready for dinner? Or lunch? Tapas or high tea perhaps? Turn the page.

Our critics have been eating nonstop for the past year just so you won't go hungry. And they've discovered over seven hundred restaurants to recommend in Northern California. Looking for Burmese food in the East Bay? Tortillas in Tahoe? A French bistro open late at night? We've got it.

So what are you waiting for?

BY WENDY JO JESTER

700 RESTAURANTS
FINE DINING GUIDE
SAN FRANCISCO FOCUS

SAN FRANCISCO FOCUS

# In the
# HEAT
## of the
# KITCHEN

Fifteen years ago, he arrived in Berkeley with $7 in his jeans, walked into Chez Panisse and started a food revolution. Now he's fighting for a restaurant of his own.

One evening last June, the drab, warehouselike interior of Pier 3 at Fort Mason was transformed into something more elegant for one of San Francisco's largest and most successful charity events — the Aid & Comfort benefit dinner. A blue-chip crowd of more than a thousand paid $250 a person to sample fifteen dishes prepared by the top chefs of the

BY BRIAN ST. PIERRE & MARTY OLMSTEAD

FINE DINING GUIDE 9

# READERS, ENVELOPE *Please*

BY JACQUELINE KILLEEN AND SHARON SILVA

All year long we reviewers have had the floor in the great Bay Area restaurant debate. Now we've heard your  side. Tallying the ballots tells us as much about you, our readers, as it does about your favorite restaurants.  You're strong on eateries born in the past decade; only a handful of the winners are into their teens. And you seem to be steadfastly loyal to the same places, year after year. Yet there are some surprise winners in the poll — including a few restaurants that have been around barely a year. We learned that you speak your mind, too. Our omission of categories for American and Cambodian cuisines brought justifiably outraged grumbles from the fans of Cajun cooking, the Cambodia House restaurant and Campton Place. Our apologies; we hereby award write-in first places to both.

READER'S POLL
FINE DINING GUIDE
SAN FRANCISCO FOCUS

SAN FRANCISCO FOCUS

FINE DINING GUIDE 11

"BECAUSE THIS YOUNG PAINTER SEEMS TO FIND NO OB-stacle impossible to solve," wrote a Spanish art critic of the young Angel González Ortiz in the early '70s, "he is capable of achieving original works of art, extremely intense in concept, recreated expressions of that which is natural, nearing the surreal." Living up to such praise, Ortiz mounted nine one-man shows throughout Spain between 1973 and 1978. He produced illustrations for record-album covers, posters and greeting cards, served as art director at a multinational advertising agency in Madrid, executed commissions for a number of large corporations and developed an interest in photography during his twenties. ■ "In 1985, I started a series of experimentations with the musical group Duke," Ortiz explains of a series of luminous photographic figure studies, "combining body painting, ultraviolet lighting, motion and music to create an image of movement and its interaction with the camera. Later, working with models, I began incorporating geometric elements and graphics, developing concepts of pictorial photography. Once the painted body is captured by the camera it becomes a new painting, how on a modern canvas, the photo paper, instead of on the skin of the model. I only want to have people wake up one morning and be able to see another form of life."

"HANIMALS" ARE THE CONCEPT OF Italian artist Mario Mariotti, who has produced several books on hand painting," explains art director Bruce Arendash of the conceptual origin of an introductory campaign for Citizen's Nobilia line of watches. "They're a kind of shadow picture brought into three-dimensional reality. When we pitched the account, late in '85 and early in '86, we took the hanimals and presented them as an idea. The roughs were visually arresting, even in their raw form, and we got the account." ■ "From that point, we wanted to take the concept to a more artistic level," Arendash continues. "Originally, it was kind of puppety. The idea was sophisticated but the execution needed a little more surrealism. We selected animals and qualities of the watches we would sell. The duck was simple and it said something about water-resistance. The zebra was arresting because of its pure graphic sense. The giraffe had a long neck and we could get a lot of watches on it. We wanted to go for concept and beauty but we also wanted to have a little whimsy, a little playfulness. ■ "When I auditioned Michael Thomas, the makeup artist that we finally used," Arendash says of finding a vital member of the creative team, "he did an illustration for me before he did any makeup. He actually drew the hand out on paper. I could see that he was an artist. He made his blueprint and got started. He did the zebra on his own hand. I threw his coat over his back and rushed him right over to Hiro so he could see it." ■ "The campaign was wonderfully conceived," adds photographer Hiro of the smooth execution of the photography, which appeared in a trade brochure as well as spread and single-page consumer advertising. "The difficult thing is the preparatory stage. Problems only occur when you're not prepared, when you haven't addressed the issues—what is it the art director's mind, what is in the agency's interest, what is the attitude of the client, what are the possible pitfalls. If communication is open between the art director and photographer there certainly should be no crisis."

"THE ESCADA IMAGE BROCHURE," SAYS RASA VILGALYS, New York-based Beckmann Advertising account manager of a 16-page insert in the October Vogue, "shows the relationship between technology and fashion. Margaretha and Wolfgang Ley, Escada's founders, worked with computer experts to devise a number of evolutionary methods to electronically facilitate almost every step on the production path. Their computer allows everything—from creative to pattern cutting, right down to shipping—to be coordinated. At the same time, Escada also firmly believes in the finest craftsmanship, finishing and quality control. We had to show the relationship. ■ "All the original art work was done in Germany," Vilgalys continues. "Marion Beckmann, is truly the creative director in every way. She developed the Escada AG prospectus, financial report and original image brochure when the company went public in Germany last May. The full Escada collection is enormous. The 260-page full-line catalog, which is produced twice a year, is the bible, the company's main marketing tool. A number of photographers shoot the collection in Europe. We then reuse the photography from the catalog for U.S. brochures, customer mailings for major retailers and consumer advertising. The dramatically different application of the same photography can be seen in the use of the same photo in the Vogue insert (below right) and a Fall/Winter catalog (below). ■ "When some people in the United States think of Germany," Vilgalys says with regret, "they think of lederhosen and sauerkraut. They are surprised to learn that Escada is a German company. Our success is measured by the degree to which the international fashion world and the American consumer set up and took notice of Escada."

Publication **Photo / Design**
Art Director **Deborah Gallagher Lewis**
Photographers **Fabrizio Ferri, Ernst Grasser, Diane Padys, Angel Gonzalez, Barney Edwards, Hiro**
Publisher **Billboard Publications, Inc.**
Category **Special Section**
Date **January / February 1987**

Publication **Boston Globe**
Art Directors **Lynn Staley, Holly Nixholm**
Designers **Lynn Staley, Holly Nixholm, Jim Pavlovitch**
Photo Editors **Vin Alabiso, Thea Breite**
Publisher **Boston Globe**
Category **Special Section**
Date **1987**

**156**

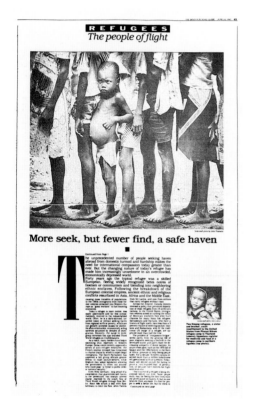

Publication **Rolling Stone**
Art Director **Fred Woodward**
Designers **Jolene Cuyler, Raul Martinez**
Photo Editor **Laurie Kratochvil**
Publisher **Striaght Arrow Publishers**
Category **Overall**
Date **1987**

Publication **Chicago**
Design Director **Barbara Solowan**
Art Director **Cynthia Hoffman**
Designers **Kerig W. Pope, Susan L. Prosinski, Cynthia Hoffman**
Publisher **Metropolitan Communications, Ltd.**
Category **Overall**
Date **1987**

## the Resolution
### Solution

Stick to
•
Your
•
New Year's
•
Vows with
•
Video

HERE'S an annual litany that's heard every January 1st. Sound familiar?

"That's it! I'm definitely going to quit smoking after the holidays."

"Okay. This year I'm finally going to get in shape."

"I've had it with my job. I'm going to find a new one."

"1988 is the year I _____ (fill in the blank).

Of course, by the time February 1st rolls around, you're still smoking, still sagging, still stuck in the same old job, still…. Maybe this is the year to try something completely different; something modern to help you stick to your convictions for more than a few weeks.

That's why we've come up with the resolution solution. We've taken a handful of perennially popular New Year's vows and matched them up with some quality videos that should help reinforce even the shakiest resolve. The resolutions: Stop Smoking, Change Your Image, Get in Shape, Learn a New Skill, Find a New Job, Fix up the House. Our advice: When your willpower wanes, run—don't walk—to the VCR and get re-motivated.

Happy New Year and stick to it!

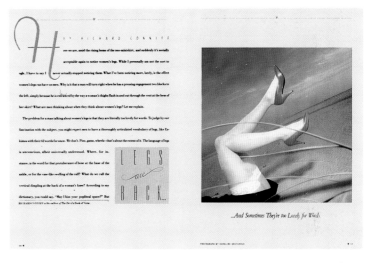

erre we are, amid the rising hems of the mini-miniskirt, and suddenly it's socially acceptable again to notice women's legs. While I personally am not the sort to ogle, I have to say I never actually stopped noticing them. What I've been noticing more, lately, is the effect women's legs can have on men. Why is it that a man will turn right when he has a pressing engagement two blocks to the left, simply because he is entranced by the way a woman's thighs flash in and out through the vent at the hem of her skirt? What are men thinking about when they think about women's legs? Let me explain.

The problem for a man talking about women's legs is that they are literally too lovely for words. To judge by our fascination with the subject, you might expect men to have a thoroughly articulated vocabulary of legs, like Eskimos with their 62 words for snow. We don't. Pins, gams, wheels—that's about the extent of it. The language of legs is unconscious, albeit universally understood. Where, for instance, is the word for that protuberance of bone at the base of the ankle, or for the cane-like swelling of the calf? What do we call the vertical dimpling at the back of a woman's knee? According to my dictionary, you could say, "May I kiss your popliteal space?" But RICHARD CONNIFF is the author of *The Devil's Book of Verse.*

## LEGS are BACK...

*...And Sometimes They're too Lovely for Words.*

PHOTOGRAPH BY CAROLINE GREYSHOCK

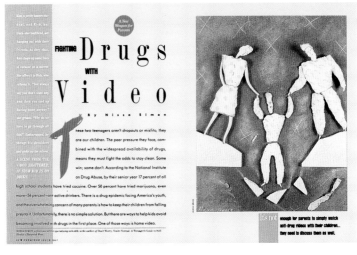

### FIGHTING Drugs WITH Video
By Nissa Simon

*A New Weapon for Parents*

hese two teenagers aren't dropouts or misfits; they are our children. The peer pressure they face, combined with the widespread availability of drugs, means they must fight the odds to stay clean. Some win; some don't. According to the National Institute on Drug Abuse, by their senior year 17 percent of all high school students have tried cocaine. Over 50 percent have tried marijuana; even more—56 percent—are active drinkers. There is a drug epidemic facing America's youth, and the overwhelming concern of many parents is how to keep their children from falling prey to it. Unfortunately, there is no simple solution. But there are ways to help kids avoid becoming involved with drugs in the first place. One of those ways is home video.

It's not enough for parents to simply watch anti-drug videos with their children... they need to discuss them as well.

The Mail-Order Magazine of Videocassettes    PREMIERE ISSUE 1987  $3.00

**It's A Video Christmas!!**
*Holiday Viewing Favorites*

**Drug-Free Kids**
*How Videos Help*

*Exclusive Interview:*
**Walter Cronkite**

SPECIALTY EXERCISE TAPES

PLUS: NEW MOVIES & FILM CLASSICS, HOW-TO & EDUCATION, CHILDREN & PARENTING, SPORTS & RECREATION, MUSIC & CONCERTS, ARTS & CULTURE, DOCUMENTARIES & TV, BUSINESS & FINANCE AND MUCH, MUCH MORE. HUNDREDS OF VIDEOCASSETTES YOU CAN ORDER HERE!

Publication **V Magazine**
Art Director **Terry Ross Koppel**
Designer **Terry Ross Koppel**
Publisher **Fairfield Publications**
Category **Overall**
Date **1987**

159

Publication **Science Illustrated**
Art Director **John Isely**
Designers **John Isely, Mary Challinot, Wayne Fitzpatrick**
Illustrators **Don Punehatz, Ralph Grurere,**
**Abigail Hyman, G.S. Grey**
Publisher **Science Illustrated**
Category **Overall**
Date **1987**

160

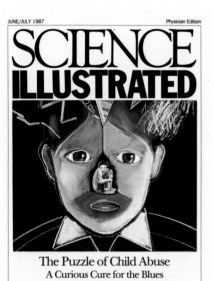

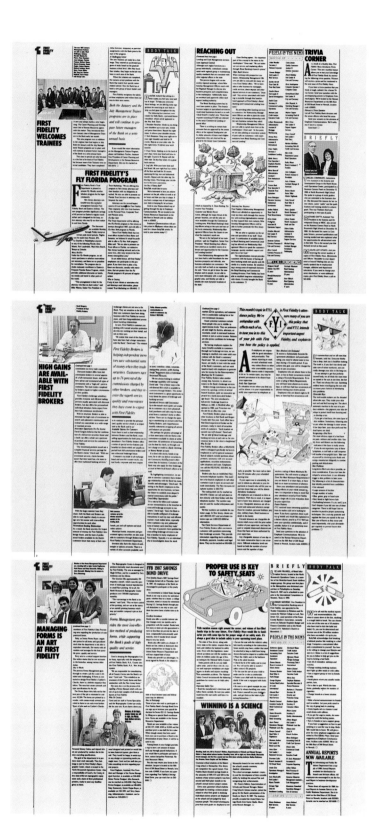

Publication **First Fidelity News**
Art Director **Hershell George**
Designer **David Gerard**
Client **First Fidelity Bank, N.A., New Jersey**
Agency **Hershell George Graphics**
Category **Overall**
Date **1987**

Publication **W**
Art Director **Jean Griffin**
Designer **Michael Liberatore**
Photographer **Donato Sardella**
Publisher **Fairchild Publications**
Category **Overall**
Date **1987**

162

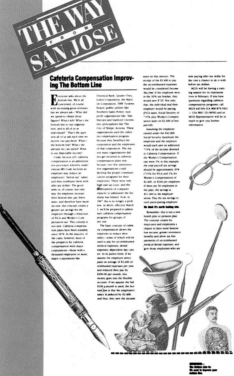

## THE WAY FROM SAN JOSE

### The National Youth Essay Contest Is On!
Open To All MGMA And AGPA Families

### Cafeteria Compensation Improving The Bottom Line

## THE WAY FROM SAN JOSE

### MGIS Announces National Essay Contest
Three Age Group Categories To Receive Major Prizes

WE THE PEOPLE
CONSTITUTION
DEMOCRACY
BILL OF RIGHTS

163

Publication **MGIS Newsletter, "The Way"**
Art Directors **Alfredo Muccino, Laura Frank**
Designer **Laura Frank**
Client **Medical Group Insurance Services**
Agency **Muccino Design Group**
Category **Overall**
Date **1987**

Publication **Partners**
Art Director **Jack Byrne**
Designer **Jack Byrne**
Illustrator **Stacey Lewis**
Photographer **Richards & Speedy**
Photo Editor **Jack Byrne**
Client **Cigna Corp.**
Agency **Design Resource, Inc.**
Category **Overall**
Date **1987**

164

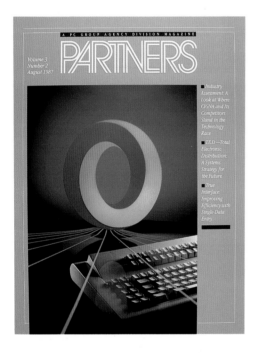

Quality service is what 25 million cardmembers expect from American Express, and that's what the company's employees deliver – one transaction at a time. By Steve Blickstein

# It's in the Cards

# THE QUALITY VOTE

*The Quality Review* surveyed the 1988 presidential candidates on their attitudes about quality. It's now safe to say that the election won't turn on this issue.
By Jacqueline Thompson

# Biting the Bullet

The 1987 ASQC/Gallup Survey shows that executives have become more realistic about the quality challenge – and are tackling it head-on.

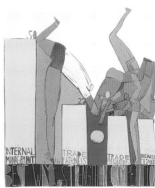

GREATEST QUALITY CHALLENGE

Publication **The Quality Review**
Art Director **Peter Deutsch**
Designers **Peter Deutsch, Barbara Glauber**
Illustrators **Debra White, Jessie Hartland, Robert Risko, Randall Enos, Pierre Le-Tan**
Photographers **Hans Heleman, Camille Vickers**
Client **American Society for Quality Control**
Agency **Deutsch Design, Inc.**
Category **Overall**
Date **1987**

Publication **Photo/Design**
Art Director **Deb Gallagher Lewis**
Designer **Jodi Boren Scharff**
Publisher **Billboard Publications, Inc.**
Category **Overall**
Date **May/June 1987**

166

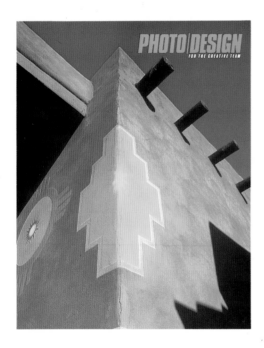

Publication **International Herald Tribune**
Art Directors **Vincent and Martine Winter**
Designer **Vincent Winter**
Illustrator **Vincent Winter**
Publisher **International Herald Tribune**
Category **Single Issue**
Date **September 16, 1987**

Publication **L.A. Business**
Art Director **Michael Brock**
Designer **Michael Brock**
Publisher **California Business News**
Category **New Magazine**
Date **November 15, 1987**

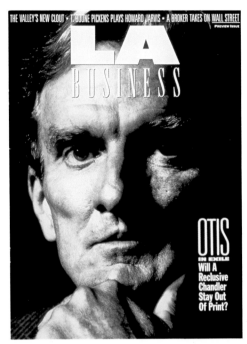

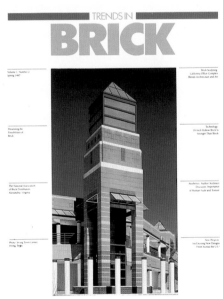

Publication **Trends in Brick**
Art Director **San Ferro**
Designer **San Ferro**
Client **National Association of Brick Distributors**
Agency **Graham Design**
Category **New Magazine**
Date **May 1, 1987**

Publication **Unisys Performance**
Art Director **Eric Madsen**
Designer **Eric Madsen / Time Saver**
Illustration Editors **Doug Clement, Mark Herman**
Photographers **Steve Brady, Jim Sugar**
Photo Editors **Eric Madsen, Marjorie Oknick**
Client **Unisys Defense Systems Division**
Agency **Madsen & Kuester**
Category **New Magazine**
Date **December 15, 1987**

Publication **Ricochet**
Art Director **Francesca R. Messina**
Designer **Francesca R. Messina**
Illustrator **Helmut Mittendorf**
Publisher **Atlantic Transfer Publications, Inc.**
Category **New Magazine**
Date **October 1987**

**168**

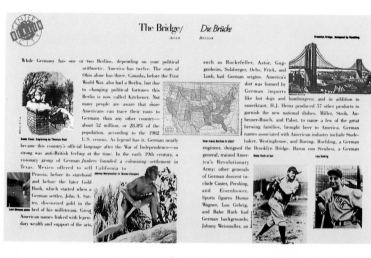

## The Bridge/ *Die Brücke*
ADAM *BELLOW*

While Germany has one or two Berlins, depending on your political arithmetic, America has twelve. The state of Ohio alone has three. Canada, before the First World War, also had a Berlin, but due to changing political fortunes this Berlin is now called Kitchener. Not many people are aware that more Americans can trace their roots to Germany than any other country—about 52 million, or 28.8% of the population, according to the 1982 U.S. census. As legend has it, German nearly became this country's official language after the War of Independence—so strong was anti-British feeling at the time. In the early 19th century, a visionary group of German *Junkers* founded a colonizing settlement in Texas. Mexico offered to sell California to Prussia, before its statehood and before the later Gold Rush, which started when a German settler, John A. Sutter, discovered gold in the bed of his millstream. Great American names linked with legendary wealth and support of the arts,

such as Rockefeller, Astor, Guggenheim, Sulzberger, Ochs, Frick, and Loeb, had German origins. America's diet was formed by German imports like hot dogs and hamburgers; and in addition to sauerkraut, H.J. Heinz produced 57 other products to garnish the new national dishes. Miller, Strob, Anheuser-Busch, and Pabst, to name a few of the great brewing families, brought beer to America. German names associated with American industry include Studebaker, Westinghouse, and Boeing. Roebling, a German engineer, designed the Brooklyn Bridge. Baron von Steuben, a German general, trained America's Revolutionary Army; other generals of German descent include Custer, Pershing, and Eisenhower. Sports figures Honus Wagner, Lou Gehrig, and Babe Ruth had German backgrounds; Johnny Weismuller, an

# On Two *sulle due* Shores *sponde:* Leo Castelli
ALAN JONES

This year marks the 30th anniversary of the New York gallery of Leo Castelli, whose artists Andy Warhol, Jasper Johns, and Robert Rauschenberg first achieved international fame. Castelli's sons began long before. Top-hit on the other side of the world on the Adriatic seaport of Trieste, Castelli was born there in 1907, the son of a local banker. The Castelli family moved to Austria during World War I, and it was then that Castelli set forth to explore literature, philosophy and art.

Leo Castelli photographed by Robert Mapplethorpe.
Leo Castelli, fotografia de Robert Mapplethorpe.

## Berlin Art
*Berliner Kunst*

A key element of Berlin's cultural tradition has always been its downtrodden and lively visual arts scene. In this century, Berlin has been known for two primary tendencies in painting. Prewar Berlin was noted worldwide for Expressionism, closely identified with artists like Max Beckmann, Emil Nolde, Ernst Ludwig Kirchner and, on the other side, the sharp, hard-edged and political Critical Realism of Otto Dix, George Grosz, and John Heartfield.

MARIANNE ENZENSBERGER

Below Helmut Middendorf and his painting *The Red Airplane* 1985, acrylic on canvas, 77" × 103". Right: G.L. Gabriel in her studio.

# AT HOME ABROAD

## THE PATSY AND RAYMOND NASHER COLLECTION
### TO OPEN AT THE NATIONAL GALLERY OF ART

# New Life In The Cultural Garden

# 2CITIES 2PARKS ONE BARD

*'Tis ten to one this play can never please
All that are here: Some come to take their ease
And sleep an act or twae...others, to hear the city
Abused extremely, and to cry, "That's witty!"*

HENRY VIII — EPILOGUE

BY PATSY SWANK

Publication **Arts Illustrated**
Art Director **Bryan L. Peterson**
Designers **Bryan L. Peterson, Scott Ray, Paul Marince,**
**Mary Asplund**
Client **Arts Illustrated Publishing Company**
Agency **Peterson & Company**
Category **New Magazine**
Date **July 1987**

Publication **The Quality Review**
Art Director **Peter Deutsch**
Designer **Peter Deutsch**
Illustrators **Guy Billout, Pierre Le-Tan**
Photographers **Masato Sudo, Christopher Kean,**
**Michelle Singer, Jim Greene, Kim Steele**
Client **American Society for Quality Control**
Agency **Deutsch Design, Inc.**
Category **New Magazine**
Date **Spring 1987**

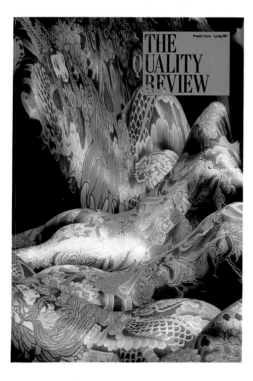

# DOES AMERICAN BUSINESS SUFFER FROM NIPPONNEUROSIS?

An irrational anxiety about Japan may be distracting attention from the task of quality improvement. By Armand V. Feigenbaum

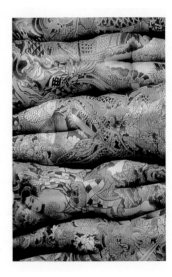

# RELIABILITY IN A THROWAWAY SOCIETY

We're just beginning to discover the personal costs of quality.
By Thomas Hine

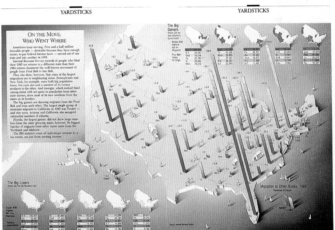

## The Mayors' Quest for Clout

Dirty Harry Plays Hizzoner

States Gamble on Lotteries

Privatization: Good Deal or Bad?

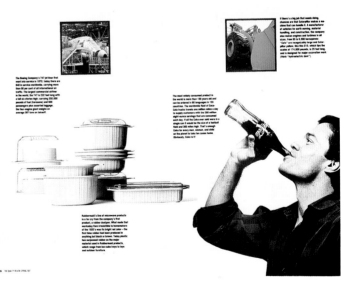

Publication **Governing**

Art Director **Peggy Robertson**

Designer **Richard Steadham**

Illustrator **Greg Ragland**

Publisher **Times Publishing Company, St. Petersburg, Fl.**

Category **New Magazine**

Date **November 1, 1987**

Publication **Chicago**
Design Director **Barbara Solowan**
Art Director **Cynthia Hoffman**
Designers **Cynthia Hoffman, Kerig W. Pope, Susan L. Prosinski**
Publisher **Metropolitan Communications, Ltd.**
Category **Redesign**
Date **June 1987**

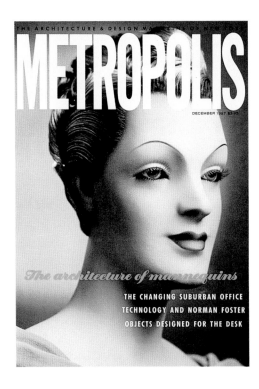

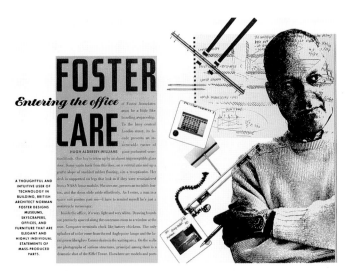

## FOSTER
### *Entering the office*
## CARE

HUGH ALDERSBY-WILLIAMS

**A THOUGHTFUL AND INTUITIVE USER OF TECHNOLOGY IN BUILDING, BRITISH ARCHITECT NORMAN FOSTER DESIGNS MUSEUMS, SKYSCRAPERS, OFFICES, AND FURNITURE THAT ARE ELEGANT AND HIGHLY INDIVIDUAL STATEMENTS OF MASS-PRODUCED PARTS.**

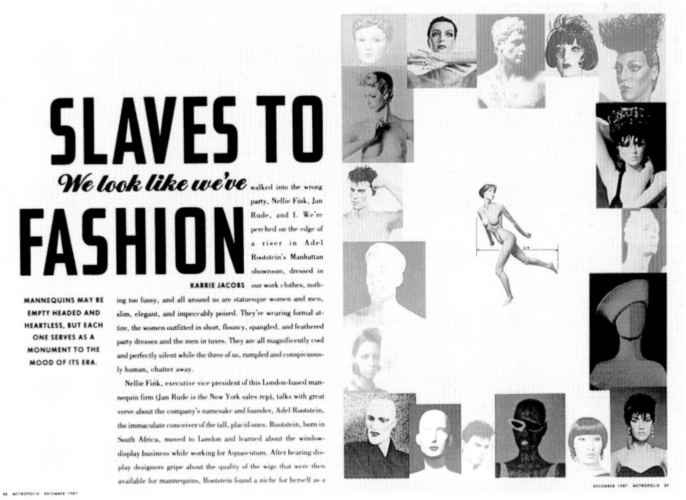

of Foster Associates must be a little like boarding a spaceship. To the busy central London street, its facade presents an orientable raster of giant perforated venetian blinds. One busy is token up by an almost imperceptible glass door. Some yards back from this door, on a central axis and up a gentle slope of studded rubber flooring, sits a receptionist. Her desk is supported on legs that look as if they were remaindered from a NASA lunar module. She sees me, presses an invisible button, and the doors slide aside effortlessly. As I enter, a man in a space suit pushes past me—I have to remind myself he's just a motorcycle messenger.

Inside the office, it's very light and very white. Drawing boards are precisely spaced along the cavernous room to a window at the rear. Computer terminals click like battery chickens. The only splashes of color come from the red Anglepoise lamps and the lurid green fiberglass Eames chairs in the waiting area. On the walls are photographs of various structures, principal among them is a dramatic shot of the Eiffel Tower. Elsewhere are models and parts

## SLAVES TO
### *We look like we've*
## FASHION

KARRIE JACOBS

**MANNEQUINS MAY BE EMPTY HEADED AND HEARTLESS, BUT EACH ONE SERVES AS A MONUMENT TO THE MOOD OF ITS ERA.**

walked into the wrong party, Nellie Fink, Jan Rude, and I. We're perched on the edge of a riser in Adel Rootstein's Manhattan showroom, dressed in our work clothes, nothing too fussy, and all around us are statuesque women and men, slim, elegant, and impeccably poised. They're wearing formal attire, the women outfitted in short, flouncy, spangled, and feathered party dresses and the men in tuxes. They are all magnificently cool and perfectly silent while the three of us, rumpled and conspicuously human, chatter away.

Nellie Fink, executive vice president of this London-based mannequin firm (Jan Rude is the New York sales rep), talks with great verve about the company's namesake and founder, Adel Rootstein, the immaculate conceiver of the tall, placid ones. Rootstein, born in South Africa, moved to London and learned about the window-display business while working for Aquascutum. After hearing display designers gripe about the quality of the wigs that were then available for mannequins, Rootstein found a niche for herself as a

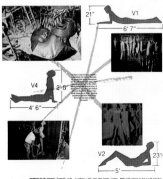 

*(text columns below continue, largely illegible)*

Publication **Metropolis**
Art Director **Helene Silverman**
Designer **Helene Silverman**
Illustrator **Helene Silverman**
Publisher **Metropolis Magazine**
Category **Redesign**
Date **December 1987**

Publication **Savvy Magazine**
Art Directors **Gina Davis, Hans Teensma**
Publisher **Family Media**
Category **Redesign**
Date **November 1987**

| Rank '87 '86 | Company Name | Executive | 1986 Revenues (millions) | Revenue Growth ('85-'86) | Employees | Industry |
|---|---|---|---|---|---|---|
| 1 1 | Estée Lauder New York, NY | Estée Lauder Chairman | $1,300* | 8% | 10,000 | Cosmetics |
| 2 2 | The Washington Post Co. Washington, D.C. | Katharine Graham Chairman, CEO | 1,296* | 8% | 6,400 | Communications |
| 3 3 | Wells, Rich, Greene New York, NY | Mary Wells Lawrence CEO | 665 | 4% | 836 | Advertising |
| 4 4 | Esprit de Corp. San Francisco, CA | Susie Tompkins* Codesigner, designer | 412* | -8% | 1,600 | Clothing manufacturer and retailer |
| 5 5 | Christian Dior, New York New York, NY | Colombe M. Nicholas President | 340 | 6% | 21 | Product licensing |
| 6 6 | The Copley Press La Jolla, CA | Helen K. Copley Chairman, CEO | 321* | 5% | 4,000 | Publishing |
| 7 8 | Diane Von Furstenberg Studio New York, NY | Diane Von Furstenberg Chairman | 310* | 4% | 30 | Fashion, beauty, home furnishings (licensing) |

| Rank '87 '86 | Company Name | Executive | 1986 Revenues (millions) | Revenue Growth ('85-'86) | Employees | Industry |
|---|---|---|---|---|---|---|
| 9 7 | Mary Kay Cosmetics Dallas, TX | Mary Kay Ash Chairman | $ 255 | 5% | 1,500 | Cosmetics |
| 10 10 | Tatham-Laird & Kudner Chicago, IL | Charlotte Beers Chairman, CEO | 215 | 8% | 265 | Advertising |
| 11 11 | Sunshine-Jr. Stores Panama City, FL | Laura J. Lewis Chairman Lena Jane Lewis-Brent President, CEO | 166 | -15% | 1,930 | Convenience stores |
| 12 9 | Maidenform New York, NY | Beatrice Coleman President, CEO | 187* | 6% | 4,000 | Intimate apparel |
| 13 17 | King Broadcasting System Seattle, WA | Dorothy Stimson Bullitt Chairman emeritus Priscilla Collins Chairman Harriet Stimson Bullitt Chairman of executive board | 187* | 6% | 400 | Radio, television, cable stations |
| 14 16 | Grate Communications New York, NY | Gertrude R. Grate Chairman | 118 | 4% | 1,500 | Publishing |

SAVVY · NOVEMBER 1987

## TOP COATS

*After cool winters' coats, which were overwhelming in every way—overly long and overly big—this season are a stylish switch to shorter, more fitted versions. They are designed to be paired with short skirts. The wraps can also be teamed with slacks on blustery days when the best defense against the cold is to button up your overcoat.*

*Photographed by Joyce Ravid*
*Styled by Kate Moodie and Jean-François Bizalion*

TOP FLIGHT: CASHMERE SWING COAT, $1,000, AND CASHMERE SWEATER, $390, BY MICHAEL KORS; FELT HAT, $100, BY PATRICIA UNDERWOOD; SUEDE TROUSERS, $450, BY HUGO BOSS; GOLD-LINK CHAIN, BY HUGO BOSS. LEFT: SHEARLING COAT, $3,000, BY MAX DOUGLAS; CASHMERE TURTLENECK, $395, AND WOOL SKIRT, $395, BY NICOLE FARHI; HEELS, $250, BY PERRY ELLIS. SHOES: BUYERS' GUIDE, ON PAGE 108.

SAVVY · NOVEMBER 1987

BRYAN ADAMS · DRESSING MADONNA · ANTHONY DELON

# SCENE

DEC. 1987

## Have fun!

**AT A
SIZZLING PARIS
NIGHTSPOT**

**IN A HOT
HOLLYWOOD
JOB**

**WITH A
HEARTTHROB
TOREADOR**

A SUPPLEMENT TO WOMEN'S WEAR DAILY

---

# SCENE

Diandra Douglas
scaling NY's heights 84

Fast track fashions from
Paris and Milan 56

---

DIANDRA
DOUGLAS

One of New York's
socialite princesses
makes the scene

VIRGINIA LIBERATORE

# Socialite Meteorite

In two years in New York she's created an
aura of romance and mystery. Is she trying to
be more famous than her husband?

BY JANE F. LANE

Douglas, in the
library of her Central Park
West apartment

**175**

---

## Brighten Up

Vivid accessories will turn the most subtle clothes into lively fare. These bold takes on racing gloves look sleek, but not too serious. $110 per pair, at La Bagagerie.

## Fair Thee Well

Lost City Arts is known for its collection of dramatic and pricey architectural remnants. But the shop also has its share of knickknacks, including a collection of memorabilia from the 1939 New York World's Fair. Hot plate, $30; salt and pepper shakers, $95; postcards, $3 each, at Lost City Arts, New York.

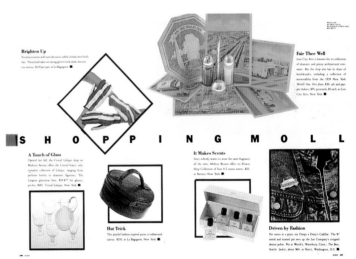

THE NEW WORLD'S FAIR

# SHOPPING MOLL

## A Touch of Glass

Opened last fall, the Cristal Lalique shop on Madison Avenue offers the United States' only complete collection of Lalique, ranging from perfume bottles to dramatic figurines. The Langeais glassware here, $59-$77 for glasses; pitcher, $285. Cristal Lalique, New York.

## Hat Trick

This playful fashion-inspired purse is rubberized canvas. $210, at La Bagagerie, New York.

## It Makes Scents

Since nobody wants to wear the same fragrance all the time, Molton Brown offers its Flower Shop Collection of four 0.2 ounce scents. $25, at Barneys New York.

## Driven by Fashion

For status at a pittance, try Ooops a Daisy's Cadillac. The $7 metal and enamel pin revs up the Lee Company's cropped denim jacket. Pin at Worth's, Waterbury, Conn.: The Boss, Seattle. Jacket, about $64, at Hess's, Washington, D.C.

---

Publication **Scene**

Art Director **Edward Leida**

Designers **Edward Leida, Kirby Rodriguez**

Publisher **Fairchild Publications**

Category **Redesign**

Date **January 26, 1987**

Publication **Teen-Age Magazine**
Art Director **Robin Poosikian**
Designer **Robin Poosikian**
Photographer **Beth Baptiste**
Publisher **Computer Publishing Services, Inc.**
Category **Redesign**
Date **July 1987**

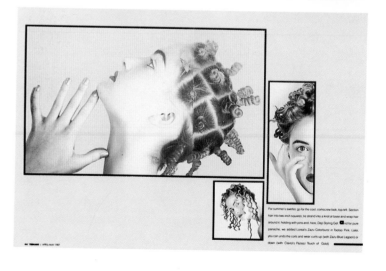

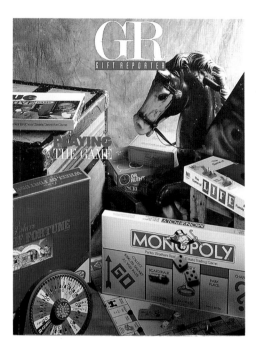

Publication **Gift Reporter**
Art Director **Jean Fujisaki**
Designer **Jean Fujisaki**
Publisher **GLM Publications**
Category **Redesign**
Date **December 1987**

# TRAILBLAZING PORTLAND!

## STEMWARE

### GR Focus

*Crystal resources are playing it safe, and the upcoming market... will be characterized by line extensions. Nobody's going out on a limb.*

BY DENISE GALLAGHER

## COSE: The Chic In Chicago

BY KAREN GASPIN

PHOTOGRAPHS BY VITO PALMISANO

177

Publication **Sports Illustrated**
Art Director **Steven Hoffman**
Publisher **Time, Inc.**
Category **Redesign**
Date **June 22, 1987**

## TO KNOW 'EM
## IS TO FEAR 'EM

*The underappreciated Toronto Blue Jays won 11 straight and knocked the Yankees out of first place in the AL East*

BY PETER GAMMONS

**178**

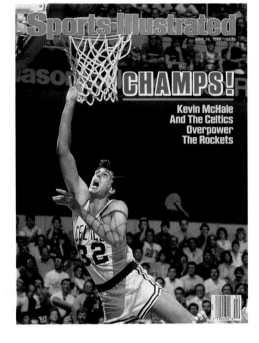

In the Game 6 clincher, Peterson had to chase—and foul—a streaking Ainge.

The Mets ran into trouble, and each other, as June 1 when shortstop Howard Johnson.

## CONTENTS

Publication **Regardie's**
Art Director **Fred Woodward**
Designer **Fred Woodward**
Illustrator **Julian Allen**
Publisher **Regardie's**
Category **Story Presentation**
Date **April 1987**

PERSPECTIVE *Everybody has written about the what of Irancom. Here's the why.*

## *Blind* EMOTION

BY WARREN ROGERS

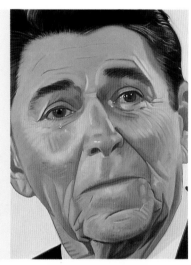

PERSPECTIVE *It was a gruesome death, in a dank, unlighted room in Lebanon.*

ILLUSTRATIONS BY JULIAN ALLEN

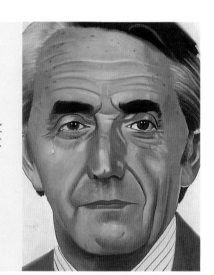

PERSPECTIVE *Casey was visibly shaken after hearing about Buckley's grim fate.*

PERSPECTIVE *"You're got to do something, Ron," the first lady implored.*

Publication **Rolling Stone**
Art Director **Fredi Woodward**
Designer **Fred Woodward**
Illustrator **Anita Kunz**
Publisher **Straight Arrow Publishers**
Category **Cover**
Date **September 24, 1987**

Publication **Regardie's**
Art Director **Fred Woodward**
Designer **Jolene Cuyler**
Illustrator **C.F. Payne**
Publisher **Regardie's**
Category **Single Page / Spread**
Date **April 1987**

181

Publication **Rolling Stone**
Art Director **Fred Woodward**
Designer **Jolene Cuyler**
Illustrator **Brian Cronin**
Publisher **Straight Arrow Publishers**
Category **Single Page / Spread**
Date **December 17 - 31, 1987**

Publication **Rolling Stone**
Art Director **Fred Woodward**
Designer **Fred Woodward**
Illustrator **Julian Allen**
Publisher **Striaght Arrow Publishers**
Category **Story Presentation**
Date **December 17 - 31, 1987**

Publication **Time**
Art Director **Rudy Hoglund**
Illustrator **Richard Hess**
Publisher **Time, Inc.**
Category **Cover**
Date **July 6, 1987**

Publication **Time**
Art Director **Rudy Hoglund**
Illustrator **Gottfried Helnwein**
Publisher **Time, Inc.**
Category **Cover**
Date **January 12, 1987**

182

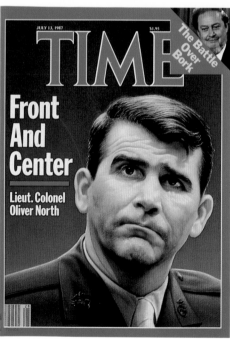

Publication **Time**
Art Director **Rudy Hoglund**
Illustrator **Gottfried Helnwein**
Publisher **Time, Inc.**
Category **Cover**
Date **July 13, 1987**

Publication **New York**
Art Director **Robert Best**
Designer **Josh Gosfield**
Illustrator **Daniel Kirk**
Publisher **News Group America**
Category **Cover**
Date **June 15, 1987**

Publication **Fortune**
Art Director **Margery Peters**
Designer **Margery Peters**
Illustrator **Robert Crawford**
Publisher **The Hearst Corporation**
Category **Cover**
Date **December 7, 1987**

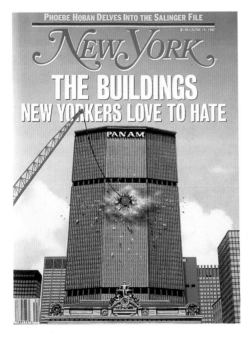

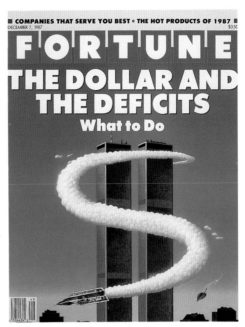

183

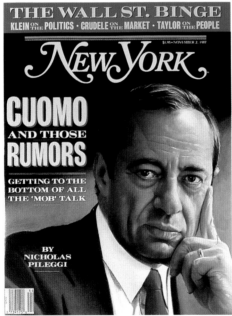

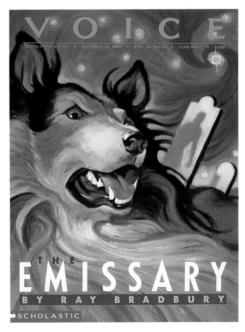

Publication **New York**
Art Director **Robert Best**
Illustrator **Alan Reingold**
Publisher **News Group America**
Category **Cover**
Date **November 2, 1987**

Publication **Voice**
Art Director **Joanne Slattery**
Designer **Deborah Dinger**
Design Director **Will Kefauver**
Illustrator **Thomas Thorspecken**
Publisher **Scholastic, Inc.**
Category **Cover**
Date **October 16, 1987**

Publication **Score Book Magazine**
Art Director **Shari Spier**
Designer **Michael Doret**
Illustrator **Michael Doret**
Publisher **Controlled Media Communications**
Category **Cover**
Date **June 1987**

184

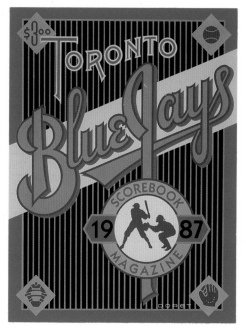
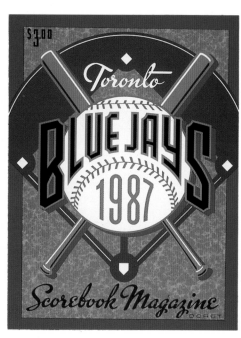

Publication **HealthTimes**
Art Directors **Fausto Pellegrini, Giona Maiarelli**
Illustrator **Nadia Pignatone**
Client **St. Luke's / Roosevelt Hospital**
Agency **Jan Krukowski Associates**
Category **Cover**
Date **February 1987**

Publication **RN**
Art Director **Andrea DiBenedetto**
Designer **Andrea DiBenedetto**
Illustrator **Joanie Schwarz**
Publisher **Medical Economics Co.**
Category **Cover**
Date **December 1987**

Publication **Hopkins Medical News**
Art Director **Tony Rutka**
Designer **Sharon Vuono**
Illustrators **Tom and Rafal Oblinski**
Client **Johns Hopkins Medical Institutions**
Agency **Rutka Weadock Design**
Category **Cover**
Date **Fall / Winter 1988**

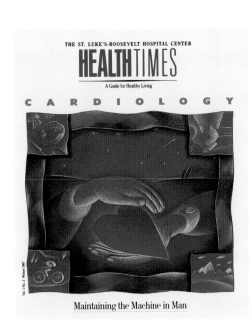

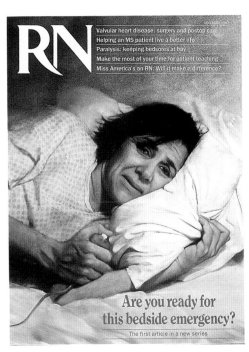

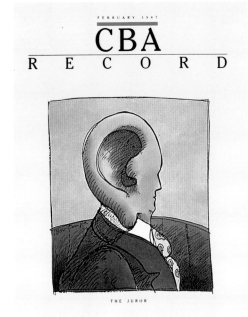

Publication **CBA Record**
Art Directors **Bob Conge, Kay Hartman**
Designer **Kay Hartman**
Illustrator **Bob Conge**
Client **Chicago Bar Association**
Agency **Bob Conge**
Category **Cover**
Date **February 1987**

Publication **CBA Record**
Art Directors **Bob Conge, Kay Hartman**
Designer **Kay Hartman**
Illustrator **Bob Conge**
Client **Chicago Bar Association**
Agency **Bob Conge**
Category **Cover**
Date **May 1987**

Publication **CBA Record**
Art Directors **Bob Conge, Kay Hartman**
Designer **Kay Hartman**
Illustrator **Bob Conge**
Client **Chicago Bar Association**
Agency **Bob Conge**
Category **Cover**
Date **April 1987**

Publication **L.A. Times Magazine**
Art Director **Nancy Duckworth**
Illustrator **Greg Spalenka**
Publisher **Los Angeles Times**
Category **Cover**
Date **March 1, 1987**

Publication **Food Management**
Art Director **James Holcomb**
Designer **James Holcomb**
Illustrator **Patty Dryden**
Publisher **Edgell Communications, Inc.**
Category **Cover**
Date **August 1987**

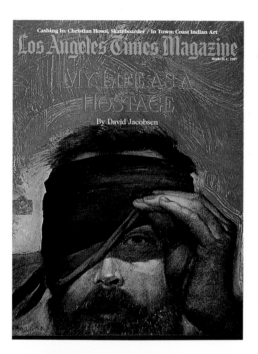

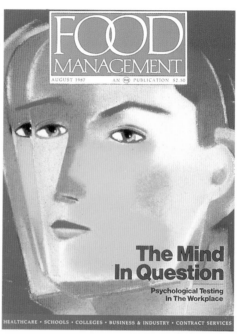

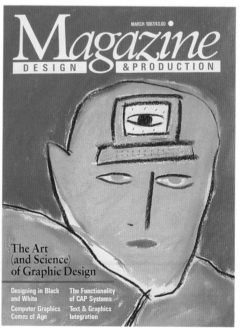

Publication **The Washington Post Magazine**
Art Director **Brian Noyes**
Designer **Brian Noyes**
Illustrator **Stan Watts**
Publisher **The Washington Post**
Category **Cover**
Date **July 5, 1987**

Publication **Magazine Design & Production**
Art Director **Mary Cristoph**
Illustrator **Linda Scharf**
Publisher **Globecom Publishing**
Category **Cover**
Date **March 1987**

Publication **Lotus**
Art Director **Deborah Flynn-Hanrahan**
Illustrator **Sandra Higashi**
Publisher **Lotus Publishing Corp.**
Category **Cover**
Date **March 1987**

Publication **VLSI Systems**
Art Director **Mike Shenon**
Illustrator **Seymour Chwast**
Client **CMP Publications**
Agency **Mike Shenon Design**
Category **Cover**
Date **September 1987**

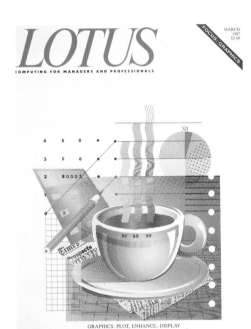

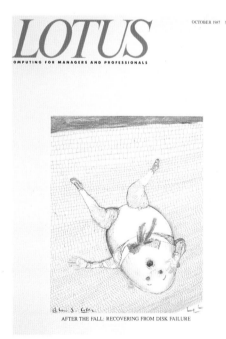

Publication **Lotus**
Art Director **Deborah Flynn-Hanrahan**
Illustrator **Alan E. Cober**
Publisher **Lotus Publishing Corp.**
Category **Cover**
Date **October 1987**

Publication **San Francisco Focus**
Art Director **Matthew Drace**
Designer **Matthew Drace**
Illustrator **Anita Kunz**
Publisher **KQED**
Category **Cover**
Date **July 1, 1987**

Publication **The Newsday Magazine**
Art Director **Miriam Smith**
Illustrator **Randall Enos**
Publisher **Newsday**
Category **Cover**
Date **May 24, 1987**

Publication **Boston Globe**
Art Director **James Pavlovich**
Designer **James Pavlovich**
Illustrator **Robert Pizzo**
Publisher **Boston Globe**
Category **Cover**
Date **November 29, 1987**

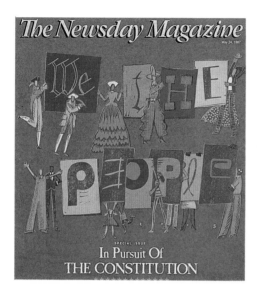

188

Publication **The Boston Globe**
Art Director **Lucy Barthomomay**
Designer **Lucy Bartholomay**
Illustrator **Barbara Nessim**
Publisher **The Boston Globe**
Category **Cover**
Date **October 11, 1987**

Publication **American Bookseller**
Art Director **Amy Bogert**
Illustrator **Steven Guarnaccia**
Publisher **Booksellers Publishing, Inc.**
Category **Cover**
Date **July 1, 1987**

Publication **American Health**
Art Directors **Will Hopkins, Ira Friedlander**
Designers **Will Hopkins, Ira Friedlander**
Illustrator **Frank Kennard**
Photo Editor **Linda Eger**
Client **American Health Partners**
Agency **Will Hopkins Group**
Category **Single Page / Spread**
Date **January / February 1987**

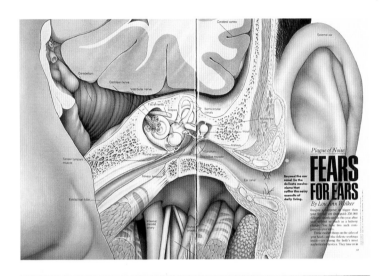

189

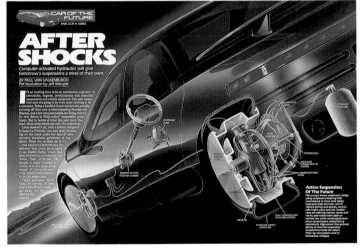

Publication **Popular Mechanics**
Art Director **Bryan Canniff**
Illustrator **Jeff Mangiat**
Publisher **The Hearst Corporation**
Category **Single Page / Spread**
Date **December 1987**

Publication **San Francisco Focus**
Art Director **Matthew Drace**
Designer **Matthew Drace**
Illustrator **Margaret Kasahara Cheatham**
Publisher **KQED**
Category **Single Page / Spread**
Date **April 1, 1987**

Publication **Success**
Art Director **David Bayer**
Designers **David Bayer, Reyilan Bray**
Illustrator **Brian Ajhar**
Publisher **Hal Holdings**
Category **Single Page / Spread**
Date **November 1987**

FICTION

My Mother's God
Three Scenes

I. THE DEER

by Anne Lamott

# THE TERRIBLE TRUTH ABOUT LAWYERS

*An Attorney Tells How You Can Keep Them From Ruining A Good Business*

BY MARK H. McCORMACK

INSIDE

ALCATRAZ

THE PRISON MEMORIES
OF INMATE NUMBER 107
THE UNTOLD STORY OF
AL CAPONE ON THE ROCK

Boston

# AIDS
## From Here to 2000

*By the year 2000, as many as one-sixth of all Americans may be infected with AIDS. How can we live with that threat? We can start by remembering that we're all in bed together.*

BY ANITA DIAMANT

Publication **San Francisco Focus**
Art Director **Matthew Drace**
Designer **Mark Ulriksen**
Illustrator **Matt Mahurin**
Publisher **KQED**
Category **Single Page / Spread**
Date **December 1, 1987**

Publication **Boston Magazine**
Art Director **Stan McCray**
Designer **Suzanne Heine Pete**
Illustrator **Anthony Russo**
Publisher **Metrocorp**
Category **Single Page / Spread**
Date **June 1987**

Publication **Town & Country**
Art Director **Melissa Tardiff**
Illustrator **Philip Burke**
Publisher **The Hearst Corporation**
Category **Single Page / Spread**
Date **October 1987**

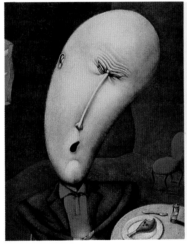

Publication **Hippocrates**
Art Director **Jane Palecek**
Illustrator **Tom Curry**
Publisher **Hippocrates**
Category **Single Page / Spread**
Date **November / December 1987**

Publication **New York**
Art Director **Robert Best**
Illustrator **Max Ginsburg**
Publisher **News Group America**
Category **Single Page / Spread**
Date **December 21-28, 1987**

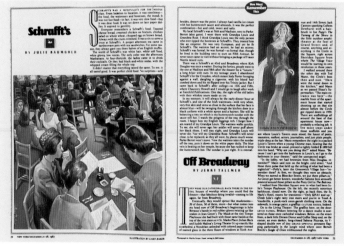

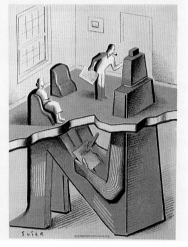

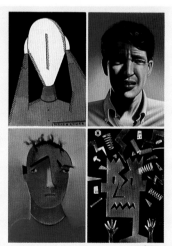

Publication **New York**
Art Director **Robert Best**
Illustrator **Alan Reingold**
Publisher **News Group America**
Category **Single Page / Spread**
Date **August 10, 1987**

Publication **New York**
Art Director **Robert Best**
Designer **Josh Gosfield**
Illustrator **David Suter**
Publisher **News Group America**
Category **Single Page / Spread**
Date **August 24, 1987**

Publication **New York**
Art Director **Robert Best**
Designer **Josh Gosfield**
Illustrators **Philippe Weisbecker,**
**Daniel Kirk, Patty Dryden,**
**Michael Bartalos**
Publisher **News Group America**
Category **Single Page / Spread**
Date **March 9, 1987**

Publication **Regardie's**
Art Director **Fred Woodward**
Designer **Jolene Cuyler**
Illustrator **Anita Kunz**
Publisher **Regardie's**
Category **Single Page / Spread**
Date **May 1987**

Publication **Regardie's**
Art Director **Fred Woodward**
Designer **Jolene Cuyler**
Illustrator **Steve Pietzch**
Publisher **Regardie's**
Category **Single Page / Spread**
Date **July 1987**

Publication **Regardie's**
Art Director **Fred Woodward**
Designer **Jolene Cuyler**
Illustrator **Michael C. Witte**
Publisher **Regardie's**
Category **Single Page / Spread**
Date **June 1987**

194

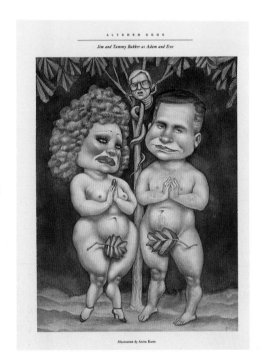

ALTERED EGOS

*Jim and Tammy Bakker as Adam and Eve*

*Illustration by Anita Kunz*

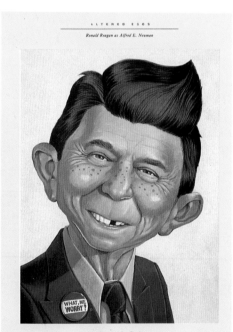

ALTERED EGOS

*Ronald Reagan as Alfred E. Neuman*

*Illustration by Steve Pietzch*

ALTERED EGOS

*Michael K. Deaver as Pinocchio*

*Illustration by Michael C. Witte (with apologies to Disney)*

Publication **Rolling Stone**
Art Director **Fred Woodward**
Designer **Fred Woodward**
Illustrator **James Pendergrast**
Publisher **Straight Arrow Publishers**
Category **Single Page / Spread**
Date **December 17 - 31, 1987**

Publication **Solutions**
Art Director **Kathy Kelley**
Designer **Eric Keller**
Illustrator **Steve Brodner**
Client **UNISYS Corporation**
Category **Single Page / Spread**
Date **October 20, 1987**

195

Publication **Rolling Stone**
Art Director **Fred Woodward**
Designer **Fred Woodward**
Illustrator **Anita Kunz**
Publisher **Straight Arrow Publishers**
Category **Single Page / Spread**
Date **January 28, 1988**

Publication **Stereo Review**
Art Director **Sue Llewellyn**
Designer **Sue Llewellyn**
Illustrator **John Howard**
Publisher **Diamandis Communications Inc.**
Category **Single Page / Spread**
Date **June 1987**

Publication **Eastern Review**
Art Director **Nancy Campbell**
Designer **Nancy Campbell**
Illustrator **Blair Drawson**
Publisher **East / West Network**
Category **Single Page / Spread**
Date **July 1987**

Publication **Food Management**
Art Director **James Holcomb**
Designer **James Holcomb**
Illustrator **Lane Smith**
Publisher **Edgell Communications, Inc.**
Category **Single Page / Spread**
Date **April 1987**

Publication **Rolling Stone**
Art Director **Fred Woodward**
Designer **Fred Woodward**
Illustrator **Anita Kunz**
Publisher **Straight Arrow Publishers**
Category **Single Page / Spread**
Date **August 13, 1987**

196

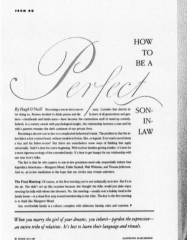

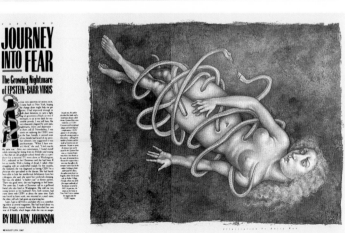

## THEIR FEARS
## WERE NEEDLESS

velyn Mull and Patti Griffith took the plunge into in-house data processing technology when their banks chose the Hogan BankVision Community Banking System. Although each possessed different levels of computer-related experience, they both emerged with the confidence that this new data processing system helped them do their job faster and more efficiently.

The source of this efficiency, BankVision is an integrated data processing and management information software system for small to medium sized banks.

When State Bank & Trust of Dillon, Montana, began using the BankVision software three years ago, the responsibility of running the computer department was assigned to Mull. The five-year employee in the bank's bookkeeping department said her first reaction was fear. "I had no computer experience so I was completely unfamiliar with the terminology surrounding software and hardware systems," she explained.

Mull credits Hogan Systems' customer training with helping her overcome her computer fear. "The first phase of training consisted of learn-

ing how to operate the system," she said. "Tom Stuber of Hogan Systems spent two weeks with us at the bank. He made sure that everyone – from officers to tellers – could perform basic operations including loan accounting, deposit accounting, and direct deposit account transactions," Mull explained.

Mull also said the Hogan BankVision System helped increase her confidence because it was backed by ongoing customer phone support. "Talking to someone by phone allowed me to ask questions as I progressed with the system," Mull said. "If we experienced a power outage at the bank for example, I knew there was someone I could call to help restart the terminal without losing information," she added.

Mull especially appreciates BankVision's ability to conduct all of her bank's major functions from customer information file to management reporting. "The difference between manual posting and BankVision is like night and day," she said. "It is wonderful! I wouldn't change a thing."

"With Apex and ACH (Electronic Funds Transfer Systems), we had to write all the deposit slips by hand. When the printed sheet arrived from

the Federal Reserve office in Helena, Montana, we had to manually input all the information," Mull said. "Before, it would take us four hours of straight posting. With our BankVision procedure it takes just five minutes," she concluded.

The transition to in-house data processing with BankVision was even smoother for Patti Griffith, assistant cashier for First National Bank in Grants, New Mexico. "Prior to BankVision, a service bureau handled our data processing services, which meant we had to undergo a major conversion process before going in-house," Griffith explained. "During the transition period, our employees received two weeks of training," she added. "The service bureau then processed our last item on Thursday, July 9. By Friday, July 10, we were on our new system. We were totally converted over the weekend," she said.

Griffith further explained that the group training and conversion process went smoothly. "The big advantage to going in-house is that we know when our work is done. We don't have to worry about late shipping from service bureaus, or trial balances going to the wrong bank," Griffith said. "We now have total control of our data processing function."

11

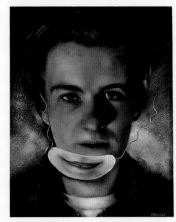

# Healthy
# TalK

**RESEARCH SUPPORTS WHAT COMMON SENSE SUGGESTS—CONFIDING IN OTHERS CAN PROMOTE GOOD HEALTH**

BY JAMES W. PENNEBAKER

n Vietnam, a young soldier named Brian witnessed an American officer coldly murder another soldier. He never told anyone what he had seen. After the war, Brian developed high blood pressure and ulcers. He dreamed about the murder almost every night. Fifteen years later, Brian finally confessed the incident to a therapist. Afterwards, he stopped thinking and dreaming about the murder and his blood pressure returned to normal. ● William, a middle-aged businessman, was caught in a financial bind when oil prices fell. In an attempt to survive, he embezzled $15,000 from his company over a six-month period. As part of his company's investigation, William submitted to a lengthy polygraph examination. Once William confessed his crime, his blood pressure, heart rate, and other biological signs indicated that he was relaxed—even though he was now faced financial ruin, personal humiliation, and possibly prison. Nevertheless, William reports being more at peace with himself than he has been for several months. ● Between the ages of 11 and 14, Laura was repeatedly molested by her alcoholic stepfather. Because she feared the breakup of her family, she told no one. Throughout high school, Laura was continually sick and depressed. By age 16, she had developed ulcers and ovarian cancer. After reporting college, Laura discussed her experiences for the first time with a therapist. For the past three years since therapy, Laura has been in excellent psychological and physical health. ● In each of these actual cases the individuals benefited from talking about traumatic experiences that haunted them. For the last several years, I have been working with undergraduate and graduate student researchers on a large project that examines the biology of confession and trauma. Based on several surveys and experiments we have conducted, we are beginning to learn how talking or writing about upsetting experiences may be physically and psychologically beneficial. ● It is time to update the old Scottish proverb that confession is good for the soul. In fact, it's even better for the body.

12

13

197

Publication **Bankvision**
Art Director **Bryan L. Peterson**
Designer **Scott Paramski**
Illustrator **Bryan L. Peterson**
Client **Hogan Systems**
Agency **Peterson & Company**
Category **Single Page / Spread**
Date **December 1987**

Publication **SMU Mustang**
Art Director **Bryan L. Peterson**
Designer **Bryan L. Peterson**
Illustrator **Tom Dolphens**
Client **Southern Methodist University**
Category **Single Page / Spread**
Date **Spring 1987**

Publication **Consumer Electronics Monthly**
Art Director **David Armario**
Designer **David Armario**
Illustrator **Jamie Bennett**
Publisher **International Thomson Publishers**
Category **Single Page / Spread**
Date **January 1987**

Publication **GQ**
Art Director **Mary Shanahan**
Designer **Anna Demchick**
Illustrator **Barbara Nessim**
Publisher **Conde Nast Publications**
Category **Single Page / Spread**
Date **January 28, 1988**

Publication **Systems**
Art Director **Barbara Cohen**
Designer **Barbara Cohen**
Illustrator **David Suter**
Publisher **IBM Corporation**
Category **Single Page / Spread**
Date **October 1987**

Publication **Spectrum**
Art Director **Jeff Gold**
Designer **Jeff Gold**
Illustrator **Robbie Marantz**
Client **First Union National Bank**
Agency **Jeff Gold Design**
Category **Single Page / Spread**
Date **November 1, 1987**

## LITERARY FASHION

### An Elegant Excursion

Publication **The New York Times Magazine**
Art Director **Diana LaGuardia**
Designer **Audrone Razgaitis**
Illustrator **Terry Widener**
Publisher **The New York Times**
Category **Single Page / Spread**
Date **November 8, 1987**

Publication **The Wall Street Journal / Special Reports**
Art Director **Joe Dizney**
Designer **Joe Dizney**
Illustrator **Stephen Alcorn**
Publisher **Dow Jones & Company, Inc.**
Category **Single Page / Spread**
Date **April 24, 1987**

Publication **The New York Times Magazine / Business World**
Art Director **Mitch Shostak**
Designer **Mitch Shostak**
Design Director **Tom Bodkin**
Illustrator **Alan E. Cober**
Publisher **The New York Times**
Category **Single Page / Spread**
Date **November 29, 1987**

Publication **The Wall Street Journal / Special Reports**
Art Director **Joe Dizney**
Designer **Joe Dizney**
Illustrator **Bill Russell**
Publisher **Dow Jones & Company, Inc.**
Category **Single Page / Spread**
Date **December 4, 1987**

Publication **The New York Times / Op-Ed**

Art Director **Jerelle Kraus**

Designer **Jerelle Kraus**

Illustrator **Marshall Arisman**

Publisher **The New York Times**

Category **Single Page / Spread**

Date **May 1, 1987**

Publication **The New York Times / Op-Ed**

Art Director **Jerelle Kraus**

Designer **Jerelle Kraus**

Illustrator **Horacio Fidel Cardo**

Publisher **The New York Times**

Category **Single Page / Spread**

Date **December 22, 1987**

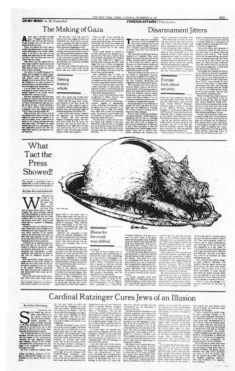

Publication **The New York Times / Op-Ed**

Art Director **Jerelle Kraus**

Designer **Jerelle Kraus**

Illustrator **Horacio Fidel Cardo**

Publisher **The New York Times**

Category **Single Page / Spread**

Date **February 1, 1987**

Publication **The New York Times / Op-Ed**

Art Director **Jerelle Kraus**

Designer **Jerelle Kraus**

Illustrator **Horacio Fidel Cardo**

Publisher **The New York Times**

Category **Single Page / Spread**

Date **July 19, 1988**

# Manners
## FOR THE EIGHTIES

*How to Master The Daily Dance of Life in New York*

**By GIGI MAHON**

ALKING BUSINESS AT A DINNER PARTY IS NOT BAD MANNERS PER SE, BUT IGNORING THE PEOPLE TRAPPED IN YOUR CONVERSATION IS A DEFINITIVE MARK OF A CLASSIC BORE.

### MANNERS FOR THE EIGHTIES

The only gentle way to learn of someone's sexual past is to get to know him or her in a close, caring relationship.

EVERYONE HAS THE RIGHT TO OBJECT POLITELY TO CIGAR SMOKE, AND IN ANY CASE, NO GENTLEMAN SHOULD EVER LIGHT UP IN A ROOM WITH NO WINDOWS.

### MANNERS FOR THE EIGHTIES

It's up to parents to make sure children's birthday parties don't become facsimile auditions for The Price Is Right.

THE TRADITIONAL RULE FOR HAILING A CAB ON A CROWDED STREET VIOLATES COMMON COURTESY.

THE CHORUS OF PEOPLE SPEAKING UP AGAINST MISBEHAVIOR HAS A USEFUL DETERRENT EFFECT.

Publication **New York**
Art Director **Robert Best**
Designer **Josh Gosfield**
Illustrator **Brian Cronin**
Publisher **News Group America**
Category **Story Presentation**
Date **December 14, 1987**

Publication **Regardie's**
Art Director **Rip Georges**
Illustrator **Marshall Arisman**
Publisher **Regardie's**
Category **Story Presentation**
Date **October 1987**

202

### IN THE BELLY OF THE BEAST

# POWER
## SITS AT ANOTHER TABLE
**OBSERVATIONS ON THE BUSINESS OF POWER**

BY EARL SHORRIS

THERE ARE NO DRAWS IN GAMES OF POWER.

PEOPLE DO THINGS FOR THE POWERFUL;
THEY DO NOT WAIT TO BE ASKED.

POWER DOES NOT KILL; IT PERMITS SUICIDE.

A MAN OFFERS ME A GIFT.
I HAVE POWER OVER HIM, UNLESS I ACCEPT THE GIFT.
I POINT OUT INDIRECTLY THAT IT IS IMMORAL IN BUSINESS
TO ACCEPT SUCH GIFTS, AND I DO NOT ACCEPT THE GIFT.
NOW I HAVE POWER OVER HIM IN TWO AREAS.

ALL FLATTERERS ARE LACKEYS.

THERE IS NO BETTER WAY TO FLAUNT ONE'S POWER
THAN TO ATTEMPT TO APPEAR EQUAL WHEN
DEALING WITH THE POWERLESS.

### IN THE BELLY OF THE BEAST

WEAKNESS CARPS; POWER CRUSHES.

THERE IS NO POWER WITHOUT ARROGANCE,
HOWEVER SUBTLE.

THE COLOR OF POWER IS DARK GRAY.

POWER LIES IN WAIT.
THE LION NEED NOT ATTACK TO DIFFERENTIATE ITSELF
FROM THE LAMB; THE POSSIBILITY OF THE LION
IS SUFFICIENT.

POWER INTERRUPTS.

POWER CANNOT BE SECURED WITH KINDNESS.

THE MOST POWERFUL NAMES IN INTELLECTUAL ARGUMENT
ARE THOSE THAT ARE RECOGNIZED BUT NOT KNOWN.

HURRIED SPEECH IS A FORM OF DEFERENCE.

CONSPICUOUS POWER IS VULNERABLE.

IN THE CITY, POWER WALKS;
TAXIS ARE FOR THOSE WHO MEET OTHER MEN'S SCHEDULES.

THERE IS NO POWER IN A SMALL ROOM.

### IN THE BELLY OF THE BEAST

A METAPHOR:
TO MAINTAIN ONE'S POWER, ONE WILL EVENTUALLY
BE REQUIRED TO KILL A FRIEND.

CITIES PROMOTE ONE'S SENSE OF POWER
BECAUSE THEY PROTECT THE EGO FROM THE VAST SCALE
OF NATURE.

TO RECOGNIZE VIRTUE IN AN UNDERLING IS AN ACT OF POWER.

UNDERLINGS SPECULATE ABOUT THE POWERFUL,
BUT THE POWERFUL DISCUSS UNDERLINGS IN FULL KNOWLEDGE
OF THE SITUATION.

ONE LOSES THE SENSE OF POWER OVER OTHERS.
TO FEEL POWER, IT MUST BE CONSTANTLY INCREASED.

EVIL IS ASCRIBED TO THE POWERFUL
BECAUSE THEY ARE UNKNOWN; IT IS THE WEAPON AGAINST THEM.

THE EXPRESSION OF A COMPLEX OF IDEAS,
EVEN IF IT IS INCORRECT OR INCOHERENT, GIVES ONE POWER
OVER HIS AUDIENCE.

THIS LIFE KNEELS BEFORE THE NEXT.

**Earl Shorris** is the author of The Oppressed Middle: Scenes from Corporate Life and other works of fiction and nonfiction. The material in this feature has been adapted from Power Sits at Another Table. © 1986 by Earl Shorris. Reprinted by permission of Fireside Books.

The Washington Post Magazine

# Revenge of the DUPES

*Every lie demands a dupe, and dupes get even*

BY WALT HARRINGTON

**1987** *THE YEAR OF THE LYING DANGEROUSLY*

This is what modern people have sadly concluded: Greed is the universal motive, sincerity is a pose, honesty is for chumps, altruism is selfishness with a neurotic twist, and morality is for kids and saints and fools.

Is it so outrageous to expect leaders a standard of truth that is at least as demanding as the standard friends expect of each other? Friendship works on trust, and so does a nation.

ILLUSTRATIONS BY ANITA KUNZ

203

Publication **The Washington Post Magazine**
Art Director **Brian Noyes**
Designer **Brian Noyes**
Illustrator **Anita Kunz**
Publisher **The Washington Post**
Category **Story Presentation**
Date **December 27, 1987**

Publication **The New York Times Magazine**
Art Director **Diana LaGuardia**
Designer **Audrone Razgaitis**
Illustrator **Michael Paraskevas**
Publisher **The New York Times**
Category **Story Presentation**
Date **June 21, 1987**

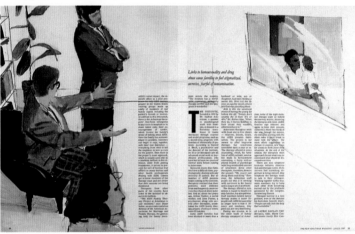

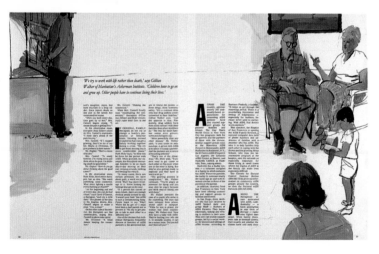

Publication **Photo / Design**
Art Director **Deborah Gallagher Lewis**
Photographer **Albert Porter**
Publisher **Billboard Publications, Inc.**
Category **Cover**
Date **January / February 1987**

206

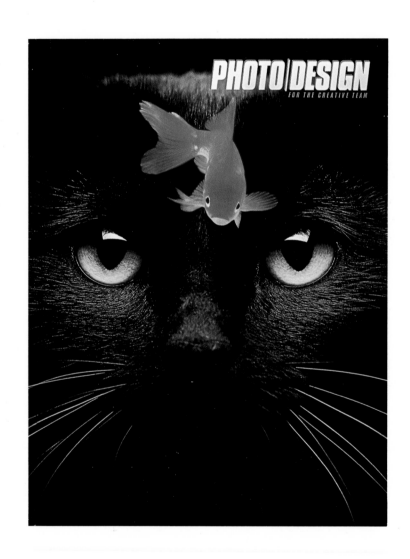

# AN EPIC STRUGGLE FOR GOLD

I t is a staggering scene, seeming to belong in a time in which slaves built monumental works for pharaohs and kings. The ancient, frenzied dream of gold has thrown 400,000 people across the wilderness of Brazil. Digging in the Amazon forests, diving into rivers and gnawing at mountainsides, they move with the cries, sweats and rumors of new ores. Serra Pelada, in the northern state of Pará, is the largest and richest of these improvised mines. Since a peasant found the first nuggets there in 1980, a mountain has been reduced to a hollow 600 feet deep and half a mile wide. It has yielded 42 tons of gold. Barefoot, bareheaded and seared, aerobic, 100,000 people now live alongside the pit. On the following pages, photographer Sebastião Salgado provides a startling image of Serra Pelada, where fortune-seekers have turned a mountain on their backs.

Portfolio by Sebastião Salgado
Text by Marlise Simons

**MOVING A MOUNTAIN** on their backs, Brazilian laborers have gouged out 42 tons of gold at Serra Pelada.

**A CAST OF THOUSANDS** swarms amid Serra Pelada (following page.)

T he Serra Pelada mine is divided into 6,400 small claims whose owners glean most of the profits. An elected committee administers the mine and the town; it has so far accredited 61,000 workers. Laborers, who are paid a miserable daily wage, often receive a small percentage of their finds. The mine is being worked entirely by hand. And it is constantly changing its shape as laborers carve out the pits, wash the earth and haul it up to be discarded or plundered. The sound of Serra Pelada is a persistent, workaday hum, punctuated at times — when the land slides, when a worker falls, a fight breaks out or someone strikes gold — by screams.

**PANNING** for gold, Brazilian miners hardly differ from the 49'ers in California over a century ago.

**BAILING** pails of earth from the crater earns laborers a daily wage and, perhaps, a percentage of their finds.

**STEP BY STEP**, workers ascend crude wooden ladders, left, to haul their loads out of the 600-foot-deep pit.

T he gold rush is hot with controversy. Prospectors say they like the freedom and remoteness. But their world, a squalid site built around battle labor and luck, has spawned an increase in cases of hepatitis, tuberculosis and malaria. And people have been killed in accidents and in violence erupting from rivalries over claims. There are other problems. Ecologists have denounced the contamination of creeks and rivers by the large amounts of mercury used by miners to separate gold from the ore. Independent prospectors, who roam the gold fields to buy nuggets, reportedly have smuggled large quantities abroad. Politicians and judges are said to have been paid off to overlook wrongdoing. Mining companies, feeling their interests threatened, have urged the government to protect their so-worked claims. But the gold seekers have pressed hard: bits of the rights of land owners, invading and exploring wherever they can. "To stake here is the right of every Brazilian to get a share of the riches of the country," said Jose Resende, a Serra Pelada prospector. "To sit on gold, and maybe touch it, maybe not, it drives people mad."

**BACK-BREAKING** labor has not deterred 400,000 Brazilians from joining the wilderness gold rush since a peasant found the first nugget in 1980.

THE NEW YORK TIMES MAGAZINE JUNE 7, 1987

Publication **The New York Times Magazine**
Art Director **Diana LaGuardia**
Designer **Janet Froelich**
Photographer **Sebastiao Salgado**
Photo Editor **Kathy Ryan**
Publisher **The New York Times**
Category **Story Presentation**
Date **June 7, 1987**

Publication **Rolling Stone**
Art Director **Fred Woodward**
Designers **Jolene Cuyler, Raul Martinez**
Photographers **Hiro, Annie Leibovitz**
Photo Editor **Laurie Kratochvil**
Publisher **Straight Arrow Publishers**
Category **Single Issue XXth Anniversary**
Date **November 5 - December 10, 1987**

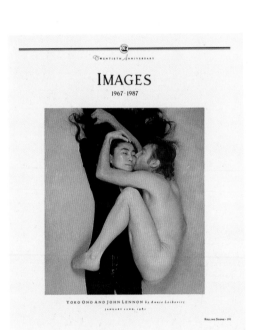

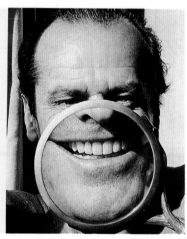

Publication **The New York Time Magazine**
Art Director **Diana LaGuardia**
Designer **Kevin McPhee**
Photographer **Karen Kuehn**
Photo Editor **Kathy Ryan**
Publisher **The New York Times**
Category **Single Page / Spread**
Date **November 29, 1987**

# WILLIAM WEGMAN
## The Artist and His Dog

Publication **Photo Metro**
Designer **Henry Brimmer**
Photographer **Charly Franklin**
Publisher **Photo Metro**
Category **Cover**
Date **September 1987**

Publication **H.J. Heinz Company Annual Report**
Art Director **Bennett Robinson**
Photographer **Rodney Smith**
Client **H.J. Heinz Company**
Agency **Corporate Graphics, Inc.**
Category **Single Page / Spread**
Date **July 1987**

Publication **Elle**
Art Director **Phyllis Schefer**
Designer **Regis Pagniez**
Photographer **Gilles Bensimon**
Publisher **Murdoch / Hachette**
Publication Director **Regis Pagniez**
Category **Cover**
Date **December 1987**

Publication **Elle**
Art Director **Phyllis Schefer**
Designer **Phyllis Schefer**
Photographer **Gilles Bensimon**
Publisher **Murdoch / Hachette**
Publication Director **Regis Pagniez**
Category **Cover**
Date **August 1987**

Publication **Elle**
Art Director **Phyllis Schefer**
Designer **Phyllis Schefer**
Photographer **Steven Silverstein**
Publisher **Murdoch / Hachette**
Publication Director **Regis Pagniez**
Category **Cover**
Date **July 1987**

Publication **Elle**
Art Director **Phyllis Schefer**
Designer **Phyllis Schefer**
Photographer **Oliviero Toscani**
Publisher **Murdoch / Hatchette**
Publication Director **Regis Pagniez**
Category **Cover**
Date **September 1987**

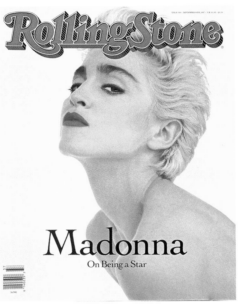

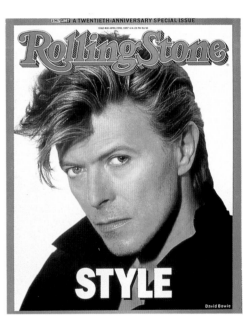

Publication **Rolling Stone**
Art Director **Fred Woodward**
Designer **Fred Woodward**
Photographer **Matthew Rolston**
Photo Editor **Laurie Kratochvil**
Publisher **Striaght Arrow Publishers**
Category **Cover**
Date **October 8, 1987**

Publication **Rolling Stone**
Art Director **Fred Woodward**
Designer **Fred Woodward**
Photographer **Herb Ritts**
Photo Editor **Laurie Kratochvil**
Publisher **Straight Arrow Publishers**
Category **Cover**
Date **September 10, 1987**

Publication **Rolling Stone**
Art Director **Derek Ungless**
Designer **Derek Ungless**
Photographer **Herb Ritts**
Photo Editor **Laurie Kratochvil**
Publisher **Straight Arrow Publishers**
Category **Cover**
Date **April 23, 1987**

Publication **Photo/Design**
Art Director **Deborah Gallagher Lewis**
Photographer **Jan Bengtssion**
Publisher **Billboard Publications, Inc.**
Category **Cover**
Date **September/October 1987**

Publication **The New York Times Magazine**
Art Director **Diana LaGuardia**
Designer **Diana LaGuardia**
Photographer **Julio Donoso**
Photo Editor **Kathy Ryan**
Publisher **The New York Times**
Category **Cover**
Date **September 20, 1987**

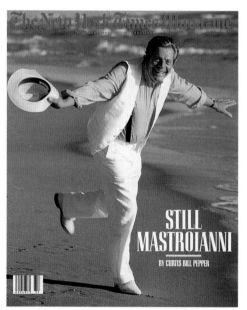

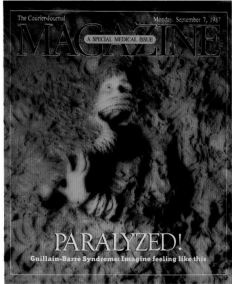

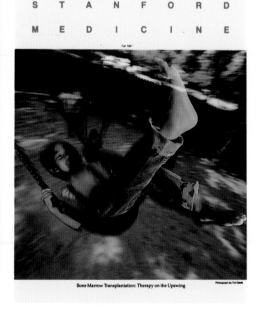

Publication **The Courier-Journal Magazine**
Art Director **Stephen D. Sebree**
Designer **Stephen D. Sebree**
Photographer **Gary S. Chapman**
Publisher **The Courier-Journal**
Category **Cover**
Date **September 7, 1987**

Publication **Stanford Medicine**
Art Director **Mike Shenon**
Designer **Mike Shenon**
Photographer **Tim Davis**
Client **Stanford University Medical Center**
Category **Cover**
Date **Fall 1987**

Publication **New York**
Art Director **Robert Best**
Photographers **Rogier Gregoire and Bill Ray**
Photo Editor **Jordan Schaps**
Publisher **News Group America**
Category **Cover**
Date **March 9, 1987**

Publication **Mercedes**
Art Director **John Tom Cohoe**
Designer **John Tom Cohoe**
Photographer **David Lebon**
Publisher **Mercedes-Benz of North America**
Agency **McCaffrey & McCall**
Category **Cover**
Date **Spring 1987**

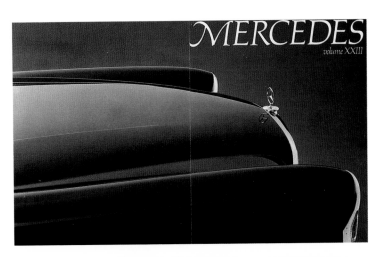

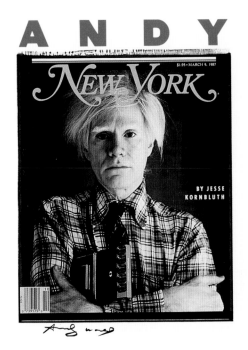

Publication **New York Stock Exchange**
Art Director **Alisa Zamir**
Designer **John Spicer**
Photographer **David McGlynn**
Client **New York Stock Exchange**
Agency **Taylor & Ives, Inc.**
Category **Cover**
Date **1987**

Publication **Mademoiselle**
Art Director **Kati Korpijaakko**
Designer **Cheryl Collins**
Photographer **Hans Feurin**
Publisher **Conde Nast Publications, Inc.**
Category **Single Page / Spread**
Date **May 1987**

214

Publication **Bride's**
Art Director **Phyllis Richmond Cox**
Photographer **Piero Gemelli**
Publisher **Conde Nast Publications, Inc.**
Category **Single Page / Spread**
Date **February / March 1987**

Publication **Premiere**
Art Director **David Walters**
Designers **Robert Best, David Walters**
Photographer **Terry O'Neill**
Publisher **Murdoch / Hachette**
Category **Single Page / Spread**
Date **November 1987**

Publication **Rolling Stone**
Art Director **Fred Woodward**
Designer **Fred Woodward**
Photographer **William Coupon**
Photo Editor **Laurie Kratochvil**
Publisher **Straight Arrow Publishers**
Category **Single Page / Spread**
Date **October 22, 1987**

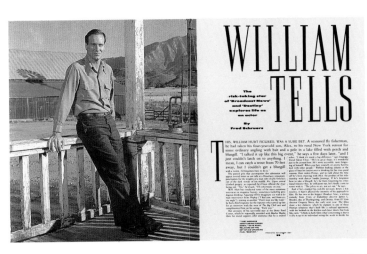

Publication **Premiere**
Art Director **David Walters**
Designers **Robert Best, David Walters**
Design Director **Robert Best**
Photographer **David Kelley**
Publisher **Murdoch / Hachette**
Category **Single Page / Spread**
Date **December 1987**

Publication **Rolling Stone**
Art Director **Fred Woodward**
Designer **Jolene Cuyler**
Photographer **Herb Ritts**
Photo Editor **Laurie Kratochvil**
Publisher **Straight Arrow Publishers**
Category **Single Page / Spread**
Date **December 3, 1987**

Publication **Rolling Stone**
Art Director **Derek Ungless**
Designer **Derek Ungless**
Photographer **Matthew Rolston**
Photo Editor **Laurie Kratochvil**
Publisher **Straight Arrow Publishers**
Category **Single Page / Spread**
Date **March 26, 1987**

Publication **Penthouse Letters**
Art Director **Danielle Gallo**
Designer **Laura Woods**
Photographer **Mitchel Gray**
Publisher **Penthouse International, Ltd.**
Category **Single Page / Spread**
Date **August 1987**

216

# HIGH HEELS

Pleasure's a (waist) cinch for this stiletto-sharp reader—you gotta feel the heel to taste the lace

## THE ELEMENTS OF QUALITY

Wherever and whenever you need a Mercedes-Benz replacement part, this system is dedicated to assuring its speedy delivery

Publication **Mercedes**
Art Director **John Tom Cohoe**
Designer **John Tom Cohoe**
Photographer **Michael Skott**
Publisher **Mercedes-Benz of North America**
Agency **McCaffrey & McCall**
Category **Single Page / Spread**
Date **Spring 1987**

Publication **Stanford Medicine**
Art Director **Mike Shenon**
Designer **Mike Shenon**
Photographer **Tim Davis**
Client **Stanford University Medical Center**
Agency **Mike Shenon Design**
Category **Single Page / Spread**
Date **Fall 1987**

Publication **Stanford Medicine**
Art Director **Mike Shenon**
Disigner **Mike Shenon**
Photographer **Mark Gottlieb**
Client **Stanford University Medical Center**
Agency **Mike Shenon Design**
Category **Single Page / Spread**
Date **Winter 1987**

Publication **New York**
Art Director **Robert Best**
Designer **Josh Gosfield**
Photographer **Richard Corman**
Publisher **News Group America**
Category **Single Page / Spread**
Date **March 23, 1987**

Publication **The New York Times / The New Season**
Art Director **David Barnett**
Designer **David Barnett**
Photographer **Charles Purvis**
Photo Editor **Hadas Dembo**
Publisher **The New York Times**
Category **Single Page / Spread**
Date **August 30, 1987**

Publication **New York**
Art Director **Robert Best**
Photographer **Just Loomis**
Photo Editor **Jordan Schaps**
Publisher **News Group America**
Category **Single Page / Spread**
Date **February 16, 1987**

Publication **The New York Times / The New Season**
Art Director **David Barnett**
Designer **David Barnett**
Photographer **Alen MacWeeney**
Photo Editor **Hadas Dembo**
Publisher **The New York Times**
Category **Single Page / Spread**
Date **August 30, 1987**

# Eye! Eye!

Perhaps the most annoying problem to face when making up is puffy eyes. And since the tissue around the eyes is notoriously delicate, great care must be taken. Fortunately, Lancôme has the solution. Forte-Vital Firming Eye Creme is so light it can be worn anytime, with or without make-up. It doesn't "pull" skin as so many creams do. And its effectiveness is immediately apparent. Firming Eye Creme, with a Bio-proteotone complex unique to Lancôme, firms and tones fragile skin, reducing puffiness and circles while protecting against environmental hazards. Lancôme also extends such nurturing of the eye area to lashes. Their new Forticils Fortifying Lash Conditioner and Keracils Mascara provide lashes with the most important ingredient for silkiness and health: keratine protein. Make-up by Garcia, using Lancôme's Noël en Lumières Collection. Mirror from James II Galleries. □

182

# Peek Performances

Life grows more and more complicated. Day often runs into night without a break these days, and many women have had to make compromises on beauty. Fortunately, Shiseido's scientists have found a clever solution to their dilemma. Shiseido's new Moisture Mist Compact Foundation makes it possible to have both day and evening make-ups using only one product. In seven fundamental shades for all skin tones, the foundation has Jojoba Oil and vitamin E to keep skin supple and moist without clogging pores and has protectants against ultraviolet rays. Most important of all, it can be used to create different effects. By applying the make-up with a wet sponge, the finish is light, dewy, with the coverage of a liquid. Applied dry, the result is a glamorous matte finish without the powdery look of so many cake make-ups. The separate compartment in the compact for the sponge is ventilated to permit the sponge to dry naturally. □

*Town & Country*

**219**

Publication **Town & Country**
Art Director **Melissa Tardiff**
Photographer **James Wojeik**
Publisher **The Hearst Corporation**
Category **Single Page / Spread**
Date **November 1987**

Publication **Town & Country**
Art Director **Melissa Tardiff**
Photographer **James Wojcik**
Publisher **The Hearst Corporation**
Category **Single Page / Spread**
Date **February 1987**

Publication **Health**
Art Director **Maxine Davidowitz**
Designer **Maxine Davidowitz**
Photographer **Charles Purvis**
Publisher **Family Media, Inc.**
Category **Single Page / Spread**
Date **March 1987**

Publication **Photo / Design**
Art Director **Deborah Gallagher Lewis**
Photographer **Diane Bush**
Publisher **Billboard Publications, Inc.**
Category **Single Page / Spread**
Date **November / December 1987**

Experts predict that bottled water's popularity will continue to bubble upward.

other, it reflects a trend toward giving up beverages we've learned aren't particularly good for us—alcohol and heavily sugared concoctions—and demanding something healthier instead.

## TAP WATER WORRIES

How safe *is* tap water, anyway? It all depends on who you are and where you live, but the statistics from the EPA don't paint a very encouraging picture. The agency estimates that 20 percent of all community water supplies do not meet standards set by the Safe Water Drinking Act of 1974 (SWDA). They either contain bacteria at levels that may cause disease in humans, or they've picked up mineral pollutants, such as lead, arsenic, fluoride or chromium, at harmful levels (for more information on tap water, see box, 38).

The effects of these contaminants vary widely. For example, children are more sensitive than adults to lead; even traces of it can cause fatigue, muscle aches and loss of appetite, and larger doses can lead to kidney and brain damage, even death. High con-

centrations of sodium (which are also found in some bottled waters) may not be a problem for a young person with normal blood pressure, but could hurt an older hypertensive person.

If you now feel good and scared about the quality of your tap water, you're not alone. Most still water bottled and sold in this country is consumed by people who have the supplies delivered to their homes. They drink it because they feel—either on a hunch or because they've had testing—that their tap water is of unacceptable quality or taste.

For some people, a local water "scare" is what gets them to shun the tap and start drinking bottled water. A report in July, 1985 that there were

traces of plutonium in the New York City water supply sent residents scurrying to their grocers to sweep the shelves clean of bottled water. One supplier sold out a four-month stock of Evian, a popular mineral water imported from France, in two weeks.

Representatives of the bottled water industry don't deny that such panics have been a great boon to the industry. Concern about water safety "produces a heightened awareness of what exactly comes out of the faucet," says William Dahlman, a spokesperson for the International Bottled Water Association in Alexandria, Virginia. "Our market swells and then slowly drops back down, but at a higher level than before."

MARCH 1987 HEALTH 37

Publication **Boston Globe Magazine**
Art Director **Lucy Bartholomay**
Designer **Lucy Bartholomay**
Photographer **Keith Jenkins**
Publisher **Boston Globe**
Category **Single Page / Spread**
Date **June 21, 1987**

Publication **Rolling Stone**
Art Director **Derek Ungless**
Designer **Raul Martinez**
Photographer **Andrea Blanch**
Photo Editor **Laurie Kratochvil**
Publisher **Straight Arrow Publishers**
Category **Story Presentation**
Date **May 7, 1987**

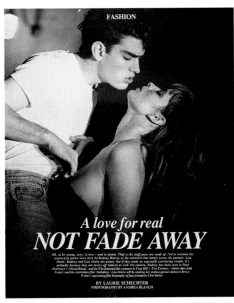

FASHION

## A love for real
# NOT FADE AWAY

Oh, to be young, sexy, in love – and in denim. That is the stuff jeans are made of. Not to mention the motorcycle jacket worn here by Rodney Harvey or the miniskirt that barely covers his partner, Lisa Marie. Rodney and Lisa Marie are actors, but if they make an especially convincing couple, it's probably because they are lovers off camera as well. On camera, Rodney has been seen in Paul Mazursky's 'Mixed Blood,' and he'll be featured this summer in Tony Bill's 'Five Corners,' which stars Jodi Foster, and the Australian film 'Initiation.' Lisa Marie will be making her motion-picture debut in Bruce Weber's upcoming film biography of jazz trumpeter Chet Baker.

BY LAURIE SCHECHTER
PHOTOGRAPHS BY ANDREA BLANCH

221

Publication **House & Garden**
Art Director **Karen Lee Grant**
Designer **Karen Lee Grant**
Photographer **Francois Halard**
Photo Editor **Tom McWilliam**
Publisher **Conde Nast Publications, Inc.**
Category **Story Presentation**
Date **October 1987**

# LANDSCAPE OF HIGH ROMANCE

Noble conspirators, flamboyant women, and 350 years of alternating neglect and renewal have given a unique patina to the Villa d'Este on Lake Como

*BY FLEUR CHAMPIN*
*PHOTOGRAPHS BY FRANÇOIS HALARD*

"A torrent breaking through cliffs, and tumbling through fragments of rocks! Sheets of cascades forcing their silver speed down channeled precipices and hasting into the roughened river at the bottom! Now and then an old footbridge, with a broken rail, a leaning cross, a cottage or the ruin of a hermitage!" Horace Walpole discovered alpine landscapes at Aix-les-Bains in 1739, but his splendid description fits Lake Como today like a glove, especially Villa d'Este. But there at the foot of the cliff lies the quintessence of Italian gardens: a huge cypress allée leading up to a grotto with the expected Hercules and framing a double chain of water on either side of a *tapis vert*; at the bottom of it, near the house, is an open-air room around a fish pool and a screen wall dressed up in a mosaic of colored pebbles and stucco bas-reliefs. The serenity is palpable in this fully alive haven of civilization. Successively a convent, a princely sixteenth-century villa garden, the home of a queen and of an empress, romantic secret headquarters during the fight for Italian independence, and since 1873, a grand hotel unlike any other.

Renamed Villa d'Este by Caroline of Brunswick, then Princess of Wales, when she owned it. Il Garrovo was originally named after the torrent, now partially covered, that made access by land impossible. Isolation and the cold eventually drove the nuns out of a derelict convent, demolished in 1568. Young Cardinal Tolomeo Gallio built his private residence there. Born in 1527, the year Lombardy became a Spanish possession

*Surprises lurk at every turn of path through the wooded hillside: urns, pools, monstrous façades, grottoes. Here, surrounded by clipped laurel, the Temple of Telemachus, a numerical bit of 19th-century architecture usually found in exclusive graveyards.*

*Romance in the Cenacolo, a 19th-century folly now under restoration. A fantastic labyrinth of Classical and Gothic motifs and grottoes. It is solely kept of sentiment supposedly from the original convent.*

*A cool cypress allée—actually alternating cypresses and magnolia—in the best tradition of Renaissance gardens.*

*The 18th-century mosaic screen of an open-air room with a central fish pond. Beyond, the cypress allée leads up to the Grotto of Hercules, by its inside are 4 Plinian confetti.*

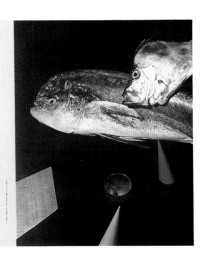

# STRANGE NEW FARE

Americans are eating fish they had never heard of until lately

By Elizabeth Schnitjins
Photographs by Jan Groover

## NO MORE RED DRUM

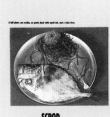

## SCROD MEANS SMALL COD

## SAVED BY THE SQUID

Publication **Connoisseur**
Art Director **Sandra Di Pasqua**
Photographer **Jan Groover**
Publisher **The Hearst Corporation**
Category **Story Presentation**
Date **July 1987**

Publication **Bride's**
Art Director **Phyllis Richmond Cox**
Photographer **Joyce Tenneson**
Publisher **Conde Nast Publications, Inc.**
Category **Story Presentation**
Date **December 1987**

*Brilliant, bold chokers dazzle a bare throat, an open neckline wedding gown.*

### PERFECT ACCESSORIES
# PURE WHITE

New bridal jewelry, shoes, and focus are feminine but powerful. Rhinestones sparkle in a young, sheen motif. A single rosette stands out on hose, whispers sophistication, elegance.

Opposite page: Pearl and rhinestone earrings, Kenneth Jay Lane. Multicolored pearl choker.
Cosmar. Diamond rings, right top, left bottom, Marcie T., fashioned of Lazare Diamonds.
Other rings, Cartier, Manquette. Sleeve Watch. All hair and makeup, this pages, Yoshi.
This page: Earrings, Ursula R. Hose, Camera. White satin shoes, Raymond T. Miller, N.Y., NY.

François Halard most often photographs interiors and environments, but here, he imagines "the exceptional moment" of getting married. "It's a special day," he says, "a mix of beauty...and mood." These portraits of a bride under a canopy of illusion, on an 18th-century bed, capture the romance and mystery of wedding day. Is it before or after the ceremony? Is the bride contemplating her future vows, or those just exchanged? The answer is left to the imagination...

Bride, opposite page: Silk taffeta gown with a peplum of petals. A skirt flounced over a hoop petticoat. Taffeta petals cascading in back from waist to detachable sweep train. Dress, by Ada Athanassiou for White Camelia, about $5,590. Earrings, Kenneth Jay Lane. Hair, makeup, Noel from Bruno Dessange. Her veil, this page: Esprit de Parfum by Oscar de la Renta.

### REVERIES Photographs by FRANÇOIS HALARD

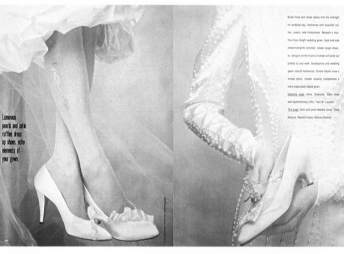

*Luminous pearls and satin ruffles dress up shoes, echo elements of your gown.*

Bridal hose and shoes dance into the limelight on wedding day, festooned with beautiful ruffles, jewels, and rhinestones. Beneath a less-than-floor-length wedding gown, back and side embellishments shimmer. Under longer dresses, designs on the fronts of shoes will peek out prettily as you walk. Accessories and wedding gown should harmonize. Ornate details wire a simple dress, sleeker accents complement a more elaborately styled gown.

Opposite page: Hose, Givenchy. Satin shoe with asymmetrical ruffle. Yves St. Laurent.
This page: Satin and pearl-beaded dress, Yuma. Kutana. Pearled shoes, Manolo Blahnik.

Deborah Turbeville's photographs are famous for their strong mood and natural light. She choreographs these elements in a spellbinding style, an artistic challenge to the imagination, say critics. Film directors Fellini and Bergman come to mind when one sees her cinematic approach. Her soft-focus technique has a hypnotic quality—poetic ambience in a misty vision.

Here, Ms. Turbeville explores the personal qualities that make each bride unique. With preoccupied, pensive gaze, wrapped in the richness of wedding fabrics, the subjects are illuminated by soft, painterly light that enhances their individual mystery...

Bride, this page: Silk satin jacquard floor-length gown with bubble skirt. Detachable train cascading from back bustle bow. By Lawrence, about $3,500. Shoe, Rikiu.
Bride, opposite page: Silk blend sheathing coat dress with Princess bodice. Edwardian sleeves flowing in French cuffs. Semi-cathedral train with crinoline flowered up. By "Flowers" by Oscar de la Renta, about $1,900. All earrings, Stephen Dweck. Hair, Edward Tricomi. Makeup, Tomoko.

### REVERIES Photograph by DEBORAH TURBEVILLE

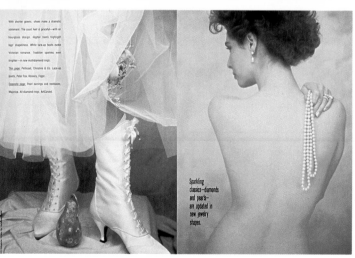

*Sparkling classics—diamonds and pearls—are updated in new jewelry shapes.*

With shorter gowns, shoes make a dramatic statement. The court heel is graceful—with an hourglass design. Higher heels highlight legs' shapeliness. White lace-up boots evoke Victorian romance, tradition sparkles even brighter—in new multidiamond rings.

This page: Petticoat, Christine & Co. Lace-up boots, Peter Fox. Hosiery, Foppt.
Opposite page: Pearl earrings and necklaces, Majorica. All diamond rings, ArtCarved.

Sheila Metzner's work smolders like mind's eye with soft lighting, subtle textures. Her images are poignant, sensual, evocative, partly achieved with her turn-of-the-century film process. "I photograph the way I live," she says. "I keep the lights low; most people are unmarried in a subdued situation. I'm very romantic. I wanted to express love and marriage in a positive way." These talented gowns also mirror Ms. Metzner's personal taste: "A lot of my work is concerned with documenting our time," she says. "To me, these are wedding gowns of the 80's, never existing before..."

Bride, this page: Ivory pulsar-line coat dress with white crocheted buttons, ruffled crinoline. Dress, about $1,987. Petticoat, about $650. Ivory "Russian crown." Shoes, Peter Fox.
Gloves, Tuxedo. Ralph Lauren.
Bride, opposite page: Ivory silk satin sweet gown with laced back. Gabardine side-button jacket. Dress, about $3,922. Jacket, about $660. Both dresses, headpiece'n all gloves, jewelry, Norma Kamali. Hair, Gabriel Nahs for John Sahag. Makeup, Major Madeline Davis. Flowers, Maledrake.

### REVERIES Photographs by SHEILA METZNER

Publication **Bride's**
Art Director **Phyllis Richmond Cox**
Photographers **Francois Halard, Snowdon, Horst,**
**Deborah Turbeville, Sheila Metzner**
Publisher **Conde Nast Publications, Inc.**
Category **Story Presentation**
Date **August / September 1987**

Publication **Connoisseur**
Art Director **Sandra Di Pasqua**
Photographer **David Seidner**
Publisher **The Hearst Corporation**
Category **Story Presentation**
Date **December 1987**

# The Mode Hatter

*Voilà! says Philippe Model. You are a new woman!*

*By Judith Thurman*

## CAN YOU TOP THIS?

Publication **The New York Times Magazine**
Art Director **Diana LaGuardia**
Designer **Janet Froelich**
Photographer **Lizzie Himmel**
Photo Editor **Kathy Ryan**
Publisher **The New York Times**
Category **Story Presentation**
Date **November 22, 1987**

226

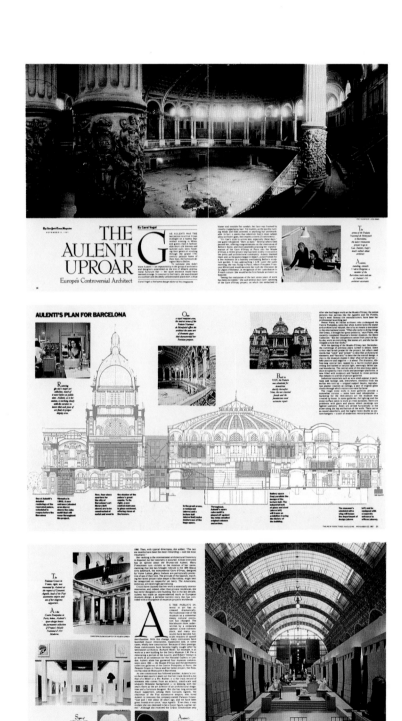

Publication **The New York Times Magazine**
Art Director **Diana LaGuardia**
Photographer **Jeanne Strongin**
Photo Editor **Kathy Ryan**
Publisher **The New York Times**
Category **Story Presentation**
Date **December 6, 1987**

Publication **The New York Times Magazine**
Art Director **Diana LaGuardia**
Designer **Audrone Razgaitis**
Photographer **Julio Donoso**
Photo Editor **Kathy Ryan**
Publisher **The New York Times**
Category **Story Presentation**
Date **June 14, 1987**

228

Moving from
historical characters
to beatniks,
Gérard Depardieu
has become
Europe's most
gifted and versatile
screen actor.

## FRANCE'S LEADING MAN

By Jean Duporr

# STILL MASTROIANNI

By Curtis Bill Pepper

'All my roles
have in common
a wayward man,
but they also
show why he is
that way.'

Publication **The New York Times Magazine**
Art Director **Diana LaGuardia**
Photographer **Julio Donoso**
Photo Editor **Kathy Ryan**
Publisher **The New York Times**
Category **Story Presentation**
Date **September 20, 1987**

Publication **The New York Times Magazine**
Art Director **Diana LaGuardia**
Designers **Janet Froelich,**
Photographer **Joel Sternfeld**
Photo Editor **Peter Howe**
Publisher **The New York Times**
Category **Story Presentation**
Date **March 15, 1987**

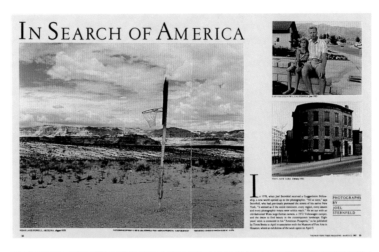

Publication **Elle**
Art Director **Phyllis Schefer**
Photographer **Marc Hispard**
Publisher **Murdoch / Hachette**
Category **Story Presentation**
Date **May 1987**

Publication **Elle**
Art Director **Phyllis Schefer**
Photographer **Oliviero Toscani**
Publisher **Murdoch / Hachette**
Category **Story Presentation**
Date **April 1987**

Publication **Elle**
Art Director **Phyllis Schefer**
Photographer **Oliviero Toscani**
Publisher **Murdoch / Hachette**
Category **Story Presentation**
Date **September 1987**

Publication **New York**
Art Director **Robert Best**
Designers **Josh Gosfield, Betsy Welsh**
Photographers **Elizabeth Heyert, David Kelley**
Photo Editor **Jordan Schaps**
Publisher **News Group America**
Category **Story Presentation**
Date **October 26, 1987**

232

# ALL THE TRIMMINGS

Publication **New York**
Art Director **Robert Best**
Designer **Josh Gosfield**
Photographer **Sante D'Orazio**
Photo Editor **Jordan Schaps**
Publisher **News Group America**
Category **Story Presentation**
Date **August 24, 1987**

233

Publication **Rolling Stone**
Art Director **Fred Woodward**
Designer **Raul Martinez**
Photographer **Jay Leviten**
Photo Editor **Laurie Kratochvil**
Publisher **Straight Arrow Publishers**
Category **Story Presentation**
Date **August 13, 1987**

234

# The King Is Gone
## But Not Forgotten

*Text by Kurt Loder*

he world is a less electric place for want of an Elvis Presley. All of rock & roll's vast threat and promise were embodied in his heartfelt snarl, his cocked hip, his smoldering, coital gaze. He was a white kid who sang black, who merged sport and style and sensuality in previously forbidden ways – who broke every rule and prevailed. Those too young to remember Elvis – or to remember much beyond the bloated and remote showbiz presence he became in his later years – may wonder what all the uproar was about. These rare pictures, taken by Atlanta photographer Jay Leviton during a series of shows in Jacksonville, Florida, and New Orleans in August 1956, offer some idea. Here is Elvis at twenty-one – already triumphant but not yet walled in by his fame – laying the foundation for a new age amid the airless cultural clutter of the Fifties. Ten years after his death – on August 16th, 1977, at the appalling age of forty-two – this irreplaceable artist remains the central mythic figure of rock & roll music. Still the King. Still deeply missed.

PHOTOGRAPHS BY JAY LEVITON

235

Publication **Rolling Stone**
Art Director **Fred Woodward**
Designers **Raul Martinez, Joel Cuyler**
Photographer **Herb Ritts, Annie Leibovitz**
Photo Editor **Laurie Kratochvil**
Publisher **Straight Arrow Publishers**
Category **Story Presentation**
Date **November 5 - December 10, 1987**

Publication **The Courier-Journal Magazine**
Art Director **Stephen D. Sebree**
Designer **Stephen D. Sebree**
Photographer **Pam Spaulding**
Publisher **The Courier-Journal**
Category **Story Presentation**
Date **April 26, 1987**

**236**

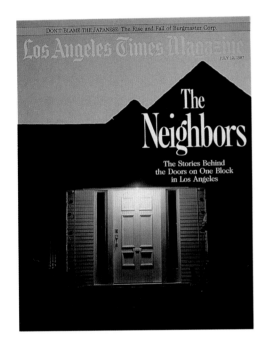

Publication **Los Angeles Times Magazine**
Art Director **Nancy Duckworth**
Photographer **Max Aguilera-Hellweg**
Publisher **Los Angeles Times**
Category **Story Presentation**
Date **July 12, 1987**

Publication **The Newsday Magazine**
Art Director **Miriam Smith**
Designer **Miriam Smith**
Photographer **Susan Gilbert**
Photo Editor **Noel Rubinton**
Publisher **Newsday**
Category **Story Presentation**
Date **July 19, 1987**

**238**

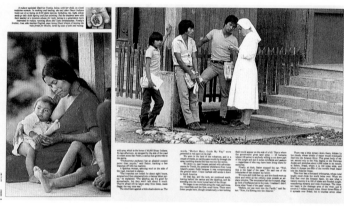

# Upscale Tastes

*Hans Neleman's food photographs show more than just yuppie chow.*

Big advertising accounts are usually plum assignments for a commercial photographer. Hans Neleman knows this well. Born in the Netherlands and now based in New York City, the 27-year-old Neleman, who was *American Photographer's* 1987 New Face pick for magazine photojournalism, has his share of big-ticket ad accounts—including American Express, Yves St. Laurent, and Snickers. But Neleman also knows that while prestigious clients are impressed by ingenuity, they are often unwilling to risk financing it themselves. It is through editorial photography that a photographer gets to exercise his imagination, generating the creative energy that propels advertising work.

For Neleman it is a smaller client—London's *Sunday Observer* magazine—that offers the biggest challenge. The magazine gives him carte blanche to create the photographs that illustrate its upscale food stories. What make the pictures so unusual, indeed so beautiful, are the nontraditional props and backgrounds that surround and enhance the subject matter. Quail, goose, and gull eggs are played against unusually patterned feathers to form a textural photograph that has a distinctly painterly quality; three types of cheese are laid out next to exquisitely rendered fruit. The final composition says more

about the artistic uses of abstraction and reality than about the nature of the food.

None of these photographs happened quickly or by accident. Neleman carefully and painstakingly works from his own sketches, forgoing the time-honored photographic practice of testing compositions with Polaroids. Once his sketch is complete, Neleman sets up the composition and photographs it using a Sinar 8 × 10 view camera and Ektachrome film. Perhaps it's this juxtaposition of two mediums—drawing and photography—that moves Neleman's photographs out of the realm of mere illustration and into the category of very fine art. —ELLEN ROTH

*These compositions say more about the artistic uses of abstraction and reality than about the nature of food.*

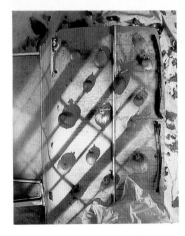

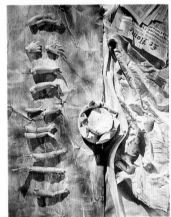

Publication **American Photographer**
Art Director **Howard Klein**
Photographer **Hans Neleman**
Publisher **Diamandis Publications**
Category **Story Presentation**
Date **October 1987**

Publication **Newsday / Part II**
Art Director **Gary Rogers**
Designer **Gary Rogers**
Photographers **Phillip Davies, Viorel Florescus, Jeffrey Salter**
Photo Editor **Kate Glassner**
Publisher **Newsday**
Category **Story Presentation**
Date **December 17, 1987**

240

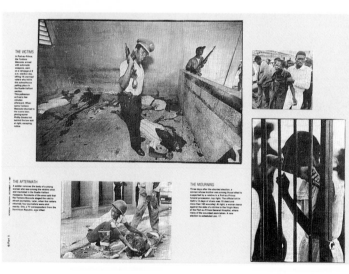

PUBLICATION DESIGN ANNUAL INDEX

# ART DIRECTORS

# DESIGNERS

# PHOTOGRAPHERS

245

# PUBLICATIONS

# E T C

## THE SPOT ILLUSTRATION COMPETITION

The SPOT illustration competition showcases the best illustrations which communicate within a limited amount of space, a wealth of intelligence and style.

## PORTFOLIO—
## ILLUSTRATION & PHOTOGRAPHY

A juried showcase of aspiring talents limited to those professionals in the field less than four years.